## CARD OF THE CHAMPIONSHIP COURSE

| Hole | Yards | Par | Hole | Yards | Par |
|------|-------|-----|-------|-------|-----|
| 1 | 206 | 3 | 10 | 334 | 4 |
| 2 | 437 | 4 | 11 | 542 | 5 |
| 3 | 457 | 4 | 12 | 198 | 3 |
| 4 | 393 | 4 | 13 | 342 | 4 |
| 5 | 212 | 3 | 14 | 445 | 4 |
| 6 | 490 | 5 | 15 | 463 | 4 |
| 7 | 553 | 5 | 16 | 357 | 4 |
| 8 | 418 | 4 | 17 | 467 | 4 |
| 9 | 164 | 3 | 18 | 414 | 4 |
| Out | 3330 | 35 | In | 3562 | 36 |
| | | | Out | 3330 | 35 |
| | | | Total | 6892 | 71 |

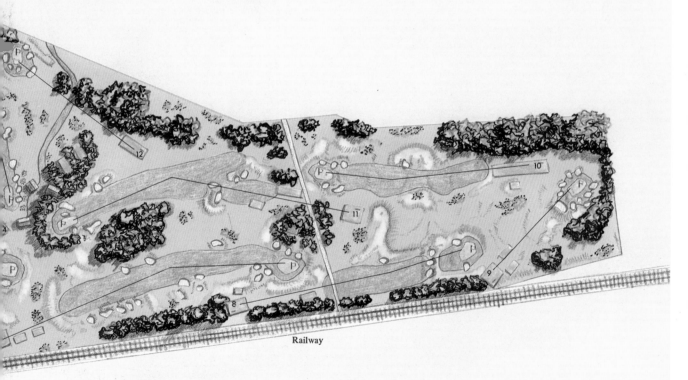

Railway

# THE OPEN CHAMPIONSHIP
# 1996

OFFICIAL ANNUAL
PRESENTED IN ASSOCIATION WITH

# THE OPEN CHAMPIONSHIP 1996

**WRITERS**

ROBERT SOMMERS
MICHAEL MCDONNELL
MICHAEL WILLIAMS
ANDREW FARRELL
ALISTER NICOL
JOHN HOPKINS

**PHOTOGRAPHERS**

MICHAEL COHEN
FRED VUICH

**EDITOR**

BEV NORWOOD

AUTHORISED BY THE
CHAMPIONSHIP COMMITTEE
OF THE ROYAL AND ANCIENT
GOLF CLUB OF ST ANDREWS

HAZLETON PUBLISHING LTD
3 Richmond Hill, Richmond, Surrey TW10 6RE

Published 1996 by Hazleton Publishing Ltd
Copyright © 1996 The Championship Committee Merchandising
Limited

Statistics of 125th Open Championship produced on a
Unisys Computer System

Fred Vuich is staff photographer for GOLF Magazine (USA)
and photographs are courtesy of Times Mirror Magazines, Inc.

A CIP catalogue record for this book is available
from the British Library

ISBN: 1-874557-22-5

Typeset by Davis Design
Printed in Great Britain
by Butler & Tanner, Frome, Somerset

# CONTENTS

Approximately 170,000 spectators attended the 125th Open Championship at Royal Lytham and St Annes.

# INTRODUCTION

## BY SIR RICHARD EVANS C. B. E.
### Chief Executive
### British Aerospace plc

The Open Championship returned to Royal Lytham and St Annes Golf Club for the ninth time since the club first hosted the event in 1926. The Lancashire links course has been justly described as a "fine, fierce and searching test of golf" with the closing holes presenting the toughest of challenges to the world's finest players.

The 1996 Championship enjoyed the very best of British summer weather with the huge crowds enjoying high temperatures and glorious sunshine throughout the week. The standard of golf was very high with Tom Lehman taking the lead on the third day and beating off challenges from Mark McCumber and Ernie Els, amongst others, to emerge as the eventual winner. A most worthy champion, Tom has the distinction of being the first American professional to win the Open Championship at Royal Lytham.

British Aerospace was proud once again to have been associated with the 125th Open Championship which provided such a feast of golf to fans all around the world. We look forward to being involved again in 1997 when the Open Championship returns to Scotland, to another great links course at Royal Troon.

Sir Richard Evans C. B. E.

# THE CHAMPIONSHIP COMMITTEE

CHAIRMAN
## P. W. J. GREENHOUGH

DEPUTY CHAIRMAN
## D. J. HARRISON

COMMITTEE
## P. E. BECHMANN
## A. BRODIE
## R. M. BURNS
## J. J. N. CAPLAN
## J. E. COOK
## M. C. GRINT
## A. J. HILL
## G. B. HOBART
## G. HUDDY
## M. S. R. LUNT

BUSINESS SUB-COMMITTEE CHAIRMAN
## R. D. JAMES

RULES SUB-COMMITTEE CHAIRMAN
## T. B. TAYLOR

ADDITIONAL MEMBER
## G. B. OVENS
## COUNCIL OF NATIONAL GOLF UNIONS

SECRETARY
## M. F. BONALLACK, OBE

DEPUTY SECRETARY
## W. G. WILSON

CHAMPIONSHIP SECRETARY
## D. HILL

ASSISTANT SECRETARY (CHAMPIONSHIPS)
## D. R. WEIR

CHAMPIONSHIP ASSISTANT
## A. E. FARQUHAR

# INTRODUCTION

### BY P. W. J. GREENHOUGH
Chairman of Championship Committee
Royal and Ancient Golf Club of St Andrews

The 125th Open Championship saw the end of the absence of an American professional on the winners' roll at Royal Lytham and St Annes. Tom Lehman buried that unwanted record and also set a new record for the first 54 holes in the Open Championship.

The magnificent Lytham links were in splendid condition thanks to Jimmy Macdonald and his team. Even though there was little wind throughout the week, the players were presented with a challenge to their talents. Ernie Els, Mark McCumber and Nick Faldo all threatened, but Tom Lehman's wonderful third round of 64 gave him a big enough lead at that stage to be able to hang on and triumph in the end.

This year over 1,500 competitors started playing in the Regional Qualifying events at 13 courses with a further 330 joining in the Final Qualifying at four other courses. Our gratitude goes to these 17 courses for their help and assistance.

The Championship Committee are particularly grateful to the Committee and Members of Royal Lytham and St Annes Golf Club for their enthusiastic support throughout the Open as well as during the preparatory stages.

We also wish to acknowledge the continued support of British Aerospace in the publication of this official record, and we thank the photographers and writers who have helped to record a memorable Championship within its pages.

*Peter Greenhough.*

P. W. J. Greenhough

# FOREWORD

BY TOM LEHMAN

As I said at the presentation ceremony: "Wow!" There is hardly a better word to describe the excitement of winning the world's oldest and greatest golf championship.

I had watched the Open Championship on television since I was a kid, and I always wondered what it must be like to be that player who walked up the fairway on the 72nd hole, the crowd cheering, on his way to victory. Now I know. There's so much excitement, so much emotion; you want to laugh and cry all at the same time. My Dad was there and that made it even more special.

As recently as five or six years ago, most people probably thought I had little or no future in golf. So, to have won the silver claret jug and the title of Open champion has made all the hard work and hard times along the way worthwhile.

It was certainly the greatest week of my career.

Tom Lehman

Cross bunkers before the eighth green make club selection extremely important on the par-4, 418-yard hole.

# ROUND ROYAL LYTHAM

**No. 1  206 Yards, Par 3**

Tightly guarded green with the out-of-bounds railway line flanking the right-hand side to menace what must be a powerful tee shot that is aimed away from the range of deep sand traps to the left. Not a gentle start but rather a rude awakening and warning of what is to come.

**No. 2  437 Yards, Par 4**

The right-hand out of bounds still intimidates the tee shot even though the best line favours that side of the fairway to open up the green, which is set at an angle and slopes from left to right. Bunkers menace the cautious tee shot too far to the left.

**No. 3  457 Yards, Par 4**

Another demanding drive that must avoid the bunkers to the left yet not drift too far in the crosswind onto the railway. There is scrub also lurking down the right side of the fairway, and the green is slightly raised and bunkered on both sides.

**No. 4  393 Yards, Par 4**

Merciful relief from the railway line as this fairway turns back in the opposite direction and flanks the third hole. The right side of the fairway offers the best angle of approach on this left-hand dogleg to a green that is heavily bunkered on the left.

**No. 5  212 Yards, Par 3**

Only a straight and perfectly judged tee shot will be rewarded because the longest of the par 3s is surrounded by bunkers, but more crucially, there is an area of "dead ground" in front of the green which is deceptive and makes the hole play longer.

**No. 6  490 Yards, Par 5**

Possible birdie chance given a decent lie on the undulating fairway for a second shot to clear the cross bunkers and find the slightly crowned green. But it must also find a way past the bunkers which guard the front of the putting surface. The best line for the tee shot is to the right side of the fairway.

**No. 7  553 Yards, Par 5**

The longest hole on the course. A slightly right-hand dogleg offering the real prospect of a birdie, although the drive must be correctly positioned on this well-bunkered fairway and threaded carefully so that the approach can follow a safe route to a sunken green that is protected behind bunkers.

**No. 8  418 Yards, Par 4**

The railway returns to menace any tee shot that drifts to the right from the elevated tee. The wise choice is a long iron from the tee. Cross bunkers that seem extremely close to the plateau green are really 40 yards in front, making club selection extremely important.

**No. 9  164 Yards, Par 3**

Nine bunkers protect this green so that the tee shot must be perfectly judged, and even though it is the shortest hole on the course, there is a degree of difficulty not immediately apparent, particularly in finding the proper section of the green from which to make a birdie attempt.

**No. 10  334 Yards, Par 4**

The start of what could be a long haul home if the wind has been favourable on the outward run. The tee shot requires a test of memory because it is blind to an angled fairway and demands a short approach to a small green.

**No. 11  542 Yards, Par 5**

The drive must clear a large hill and big hitters have to decide whether to take the left-hand route to clear the cross bunkers for a shorter and more direct line to the green. But the width of fairway and depth of rough offer serious threat, and the more judicious line down the right will require three strokes to the green with the hope of a single putt for birdie.

**No. 12  198 Yards, Par 3**

There is out of bounds close to the right edge of the green, which is both raised and angled. Probably the most difficult of all the short holes. The prevailing wind is from the left so that the tee shot must be held up against it.

**No. 13  342 Yards, Par 4**

The start of Murder Mile — a succession of six par 4s measuring well over 2,000 yards in total that will determine the quality of any score, although this hole is a breather and offers the best chance of a birdie. Straightforward and honest even though it is flanked by bunkers on either side.

**No. 14  445 Yards, Par 4**

The tee shot must be kept down the left and away from the bunkers and hills to the right to provide a sensible approach to the green. There is rough to the right and out of bounds immediately right of the putting surface so that the approach must be carefully directed.

**No. 15  463 Yards, Par 4**

The line from the tee must cut the corner of the fairway to bring the green within range, and even then the approach must find a way between the dunes and over the cross bunkers with rough to the left of the green and traps to the right.

**No. 16  357 Yards, Par 4**

A blind tee shot that must be well placed to provide the best route to the green, although Seve Ballesteros chose his own passage in 1979 by scoring a birdie after playing his approach from an overflow car park that was short and right.

**No. 17  467 Yards, Par 4**

The driving area is frighteningly small between a range of bunkers on the left and dense scrub and bushes to the right. The hole turns left to an open green guarded by bunkers on either side. Ideally the tee shot must be as far right as safely possible.

**No. 18  414 Yards, Par 4**

The definitive par 4 and classic closing hole. The landing area is flanked by bunkers with the additional menace of cross bunkers in the fairway. The brave drive offers a gentler approach to a green that is narrow and well-bunkered. In truth, a test of judgement until the final stroke.

# LYTHAM DEFINES ITS CHAMPIONS

## BY MICHAEL McDONNELL

There is an inescapable link between the character of the land over which a championship is played and the personal qualities and skills it demands of the eventual winner. What develops in consequence is a selection process that is at times both sweeping and savage until the right candidate is identified.

It therefore follows that some common trait must exist between past champions who have prevailed over specific terrain, not necessarily in their style but certainly in the process of guiding a golf ball round 18 holes without serious harm to scorecard or temper. The formula is certainly appropriate to those who have captured the Open Championship at Royal Lytham and St Annes.

The course itself, south of Blackpool on the Lancashire coast, forms part of a rich belt of seaside links, although it is now so far removed from the seashore as to be hemmed in by suburban houses and a railway line. Yet Royal Lytham still observes the traditional values upon which the game was founded. It honours the ancient art of keeping out of trouble, which was the essential skill in the distant days of hickory shafts, Haskell golf balls and fierce crosswinds that swept across narrow and fast-running fairways littered with pot bunkers of unimaginable depth.

What developed was a kind of stepping-stone strategy in which the ball was always deposited in safe and secure portions of the fairways so that no risks were taken and the winning tactic therefore was to let the other chap slip up, lose patience, and make the mistakes. Indeed, the narrative of most Open Championships at Royal Lytham followed the familiar script of lost opportunities while the winner held firm.

Jack Nicklaus needed to play par golf over the last two holes in 1963 to become champion but could not manage it. The American professional Al Watrous held a precious lead on the 17th hole in 1926 but lost in dramatic circumstances to Bobby Jones. David Thomas was within sight of victory in 1958 when he faltered on that same hole and eventually lost a 36-hole play-off to the Australian Peter Thomson. In that championship, too, Eric Brown dropped two strokes on the last hole when par would have given him the title outright.

Thus this seaside course imposes constraints that are unmatched by any other major venue — even St Andrews, where at least there is sufficient space to avoid the hidden hazards. The golf essayist Bernard Darwin defined the underlying challenge of Royal Lytham in these terms: "There is plenty of rough grass on either side and the hitting of a good straight tee shot which seemed so simple and made the holes seem simple will be a cause for constant anxiety."

Bobby Jones hit a mashie from this spot to win the 1926 Open Championship.

Accordingly, the roll of honour offers evidence of the manner in which Royal Lytham rewards self-control, patience and concentration, qualities that characterised the playing styles of Jones (1926),

At 553 yards, the seventh is the longest hole at Royal Lytham and one of the best birdie opportunities.

Bobby Locke (1952), Thomson (1958), Tony Jacklin (1969) and Gary Player (1974) at their best. Only Seve Ballesteros (1979 and 1988), a competitor notorious for his wildness from the tee, might seem to contradict the rule. But during his 1979 win, when his approach shot from an overflow car park seemed to emphasise his erratic style, he demonstrated a superlative short game, especially from bunkers, which atoned for other aberrations. And in 1988, apart for the occasional indulgence, he was the model of relentless accuracy that reached new heights with his last-round 65.

The truth was that Seve thrived on crisis and could never be diminished by the consequence of a wayward stroke. Peter Dobereiner, writing in *The Guardian* newspaper at the time of Seve's first triumph, observed: "What came as a shock and delight was the way he kicked down the door, elbowed the mighty Jack Nicklaus, Hale Irwin and Tom Watson aside, and plonked himself in the seat of honour.

"According to the pundits, Ballesteros' type of abandoned fury is a sure way of finding the rough. Of course it is; Ballesteros was seldom out of it. This game was always meant to be an exercise in imagination, flair and emotion, and these elements have been disappearing from the tournament scene." Until Seve came along, of course.

Curiously enough, the Open is never more, as it were, available to newcomers than when it is held at Royal Lytham, because Seve Ballesteros, Tony Jacklin and now Tom Lehman all secured their first major titles there; and even Bobby Jones back in 1926 became Open champion for the first time, although he had previously won the US Amateur which many regarded as his first big win after seven lean years without success.

Certainly Nicklaus was looking for his first British title in 1963 until those final errors allowed left-hander Bob Charles and American professional Phil Rodgers to play-off over 36 holes for the title. The New Zealander produced a phenomenal performance by single-putting 11 greens in his morning round, and afterwards the distinguished golf writer Pat Ward-Thomas reflected that Charles had "tormented and destroyed Rodgers with a merciless finality."

The cursory strategy at Lytham is to make a score on the outward nine then hold on to it on the way home. More precisely, it has to be protected over the closing stretch, particularly the last holes where so much drama has unfolded and the difference between winners and losers made painfully apparent. In the closing minutes of the 1926 championship, Jones played a title-winning stroke from a sandy lie on the 17th hole that to this day is commemorated

The well-guarded 10th green slopes severely from back to front.

by a plaque near the spot, while the mashie club he played hangs in the main lounge of the elegant Victorian clubhouse underneath his portrait.

Jones was two strokes behind Watrous after the third round on the final day and they strolled over to the nearby Majestic Hotel, where Jones was staying, to have lunch and take a rest. As they headed back for the final round Jones told his playing partner: "The champion and the runner-up will come from our pair."

So it transpired, although Jones looked in serious trouble on the 17th as he faced a 175-yard stroke to the green which Watrous already had reached safely with his second stroke. Jones took the ball cleanly from the sand with his languid swing and deposited it close to the flagstick. Watrous was devastated and took three putts while Jones went on to become champion.

There was high drama, too, when Gary Player, who had led the 1974 Open from the start — the first in which the 1.68-inch diameter ball was made compulsory — suddenly ran into crisis on the 17th as his approach disappeared into long grass at the edge of the green and the five minutes of allotted search time ticked away. With seconds to spare, the ball was found, but more trouble awaited him on the last, when his approach ran through to the edge of the

The left-hand route to the 11th green is dangerous.

The 13th is the first of a succession of six par-4 holes.

clubhouse wall and he had to play left-handed with the back of his putter to find the green and become champion for the third time.

It is a mark of the wider importance of Royal Lytham that the establishment itself has become inexorably linked with the history of the game and some of its major milestones. Cecile Leitch, Joyce Wethered and Marley Spearman all won the English Ladies Amateur title there.

Louise Suggs became British champion in 1948 when she beat Jean Donald in the final. Indeed the inaugural championship was held there in 1893 and won by Lady Margaret Scott.

In 1935 Lawson Little captured the British Amateur title by defeating Dr William Tweddell on the last green; and in 1975 Nick Faldo won the English Amateur championship at the age of 18, then two years later returned to Royal Lytham as a member of the Ryder Cup team and defeated Tom Watson, who that year had won both the US Masters and Open titles, in the singles.

From a wider historical perspective, two separate events have changed the face of world golf in modern times and by coincidence both occurred at Royal Lytham. The first went almost unnoticed but was to make massive impact on the professional game. During the 1977 Ryder Cup Nicklaus met privately with the late Lord Derby, then President of the Professional Golfers' Association, to discuss the one-sidedness of the contests and suggested that the weaker Great Britain and Ireland team should become a total European squad.

The 16th was the site of Seve Ballesteros' car park shot in 1979 from short and right of the green.

The most difficult hole of the championship, the 17th has a small driving area and a green guarded by bunkers.

Nicklaus wrote afterwards: "I know that national pride is involved but at some point reality must prevail if the event isn't to decline into little more than an exhibition." Two years later a European team arrived at the Greenbrier in West Virginia, and by the early 1980s the matches had become so close that neither team could ever again be regarded as overwhelming favourites because the balance of power had evened out.

Yet perhaps none of this would have been possible without the heroic exploits of Jacklin, whose historic Open victory in 1969 at Royal Lytham lifted the home game out of its second-class image and encouraged youngsters to aspire to greater things. His triumph set the European game towards a new level of excellence in which golf became the first choice of youngsters and not something to be taken up because they were not good enough for other pursuits.

During that glorious week in July, Jacklin concerned himself solely with the tempo of his brisk swing and spent much of his practice time trying to find a measured pace. In the final round he was never under serious threat once he snapped up two early birdies, and only Charles, his playing partner, kept within range but never close enough to menace. When it was over and the excitement had died and the crowds departed, we knew we had witnessed a piece

of history. Yet there was a feeling too of emptiness, and the words of Pat Ward-Thomas sprang to mind after another championship at Lytham.

He reflected: "I am writing these notes at a window in that most hospitable dormy house, looking out across a links deserted in the evening sunshine and cannot escape that feeling of sadness that always follows a happy occasion." We know the mood but it soon passes because there is always the next time.

Royal Lytham's 18th is a classic closing hole.

Although Paul Broadhurst (65) was a surprise leader, he had a history of low scores, including 63 in the 1990 Open.

# SCORES REFLECT BENIGN WEATHER

## BY ROBERT SOMMERS

Returning to familiar scenes gives us the opportunity to look back on extraordinary moments we witnessed long ago and relive them once again. In the last 70 years, Royal Lytham and St Annes, a hard and punishing links course located in Lancashire near Blackpool, a mile from the coast, had seen a number of wonderful moments. In the first Open brought to Royal Lytham, the peerless amateur Bobby Jones played one of the most famous shots in the game's lore, rifling a mashie from a sandy lie behind a rise of mounds that blocked his view onto the distant green and beating his friend and fellow American Al Watrous.

It was here, too, that Bobby Locke, Gary Player, Peter Thomson and Bob Charles, the Open's only left-handed champion, added to their glory. Most particularly, though, it was here that Tony Jacklin ended a period of 18 years without a British champion by beating Charles, Thomson, Roberto de Vicenzo and Jack Nicklaus, all former champions, in the 1969 Open.

Perhaps, though, the last two were the most memorable of the Lytham Opens. Seve Ballesteros won them both, his first in 1979 as a precocious 22-year-old, and his second in 1988 as a seasoned professional playing inspired golf. He had outscored Nicklaus and Ben Crenshaw by three strokes in 1979; nine years later, though, locked in a heroic battle with Nick Price, he played at the peak of his game, shot a blistering 65 in the last round, and edged Price by two strokes. He climaxed his round with an amazing chip-and-run that nipped the rim of the cup and sat inches away.

Ballesteros remembers that shot vividly, in part because he has seen the video tape so often. On the Monday before the 125th Open Championship began, once again at Royal Lytham and St Annes, he told of watching the shot and joked that he's sure one day the ball will tumble into the cup.

Paul Broadhurst played in the 1988 championship as well. He was a 22-year-old amateur then, shot 76 in the last round, and with 296 tied for 57th place, 23 strokes behind Ballesteros' 273. Nevertheless, Broadhurst had survived the 36-hole cut and won the silver medal as low amateur.

Ironically, as the 1996 Open began to unfold, Ballesteros and Broadhurst nearly swapped scores. While Seve opened with 74, two strokes better than Broadhurst's closing round in 1988, it was Broadhurst who shot 65, matching Seve's course record and carrying him into a two-stroke lead over the eight men clustered at 67. Eight others shot 68.

It had been a day of low scoring not only because of the strength of the field but primarily because Royal Lytham and St Annes lay helpless under calm and dry conditions. Lancashire had been caught in a long period of dry weather, and the course showed it. The ground was hard and fast-running, the rough wispy and thin, the wind nothing more than a light breeze, and the greens putted slower than those most players were accustomed to playing. Although the golf course measured 6,892 yards, it played much shorter because of the hard ground.

To illustrate the weather's effect, examine how the par 5s played. Lytham has three. The sixth, the shortest of the three, measures 490 yards; the seventh, the longest, stretches 553 yards, and the 11th, which asks for the most precise drive, measures 542 yards. Every one of them was reachable with an iron second shot. While John Daly is not a good example to cite because of his uncommon power, nevertheless in a practice round he played the 11th with a driver and a pitching wedge, and in the first round he reached both the sixth and seventh with wedges as well. Later in the week, in the heat of competition, Tom Lehman was on the seventh with an eight iron for his second, Ernie Els reached the sixth with a seven iron in the first round, and a few minutes later Price was on

The Open Championship began at 7 o'clock and Malcolm Mackenzie's early burst forecast the low scores to come.

with an eight iron. Those who didn't birdie gave up half a stroke to the field.

As the Open approached, weather forecasts offered no hope the pattern would ease and England could return to normal. A system of high pressure centred over Britain brought clear skies and a hot sun that raised the temperature into the mid-20s Celsius (high 70s and low 80s Fahrenheit), pleasant for everyone concerned but not so welcome to those who count on unpredictable and occasional foul weather to protect the integrity of the golf courses. Players comprehensively predicted low if not record-breaking scores. The weather had become so benign it worried the Royal and Ancient Golf Club of St Andrews.

Expressing the club's concern, Michael Bonallack, the R and A's secretary, said: "I am fearful of what is round the corner. The weather is incredible, really. Nick Price has just been saying he would like a little more breeze, but, sadly, we don't have any control over that."

The wind was clocked at just a little over five miles per hour when the early starters teed off, which not only disappointed some of the more prominent players but frightened others. Paul Azinger, the 1993 USPGA champion, reminded everyone that links

courses rely on wind: "Most of them have four defences — wind, water, sand and rough. Take away the first two and they're close to helpless."

Lee Janzen, who had won the 1993 US Open, was afraid that "someone on Sunday could shoot nothing and win from miles back." While the Open didn't end as Janzen suspected it might, it was true indeed that the scores ran low, as everyone predicted. Aside from those 17 men who shot 68 or better, 25 others broke Royal Lytham's par of 71, making 42 in all, and 20 others matched it — 62 men at 71 or better.

The group at 67 was made up of seven Americans and one Japanese. Hidemichi Tanaka, from Hiroshima, showed more enthusiasm than any of the other leaders, stating that on a scale of one to a hundred, he would rank his round at 20,000. Tied with him were Fred Couples, Brad Faxon, Mark O'Meara, Mark Brooks, Loren Roberts and, more significantly, Mark McCumber and Lehman. They would be there at the finish.

Celebrating his 39th birthday, Nick Faldo was among those at 68, along with Shigeki Maruyama, another Japanese with enormous power, Carl Mason, Klas Eriksson, Jim Furyk, Padraig Harrington, Price, the 1994 champion, and Els, the 1994 US Open champion.

Fred Couples was one of seven Americans returning 67s, two strokes off the opening-round lead.

Mark McCumber (67) was playing with a sore shoulder.

Tom Lehman (67) compared the weather to Arizona.

A drive into an unplayable lie on the home hole kept Mark O'Meara (67) from holding second place alone.

Mark Brooks (67) relied heavily on his driver.

Brad Faxon (67) said he enjoys playing links golf.

It was a fine day for Nicklaus as well. Playing in his 35th consecutive Open Championship, he stood among the seven men who shot 69. Others, though, played much worse. Colin Montgomerie had come to Lytham seething because, he claimed, the high winds at the Scottish Open, the previous week in Carnoustie, had ruined his swing. Perhaps it did; level par through 17 holes, he made 6 on the home hole and shot 73, two over par. Ian Woosnam, who had won the Scottish Open, shot an absurd 75 that featured one double bogey, one eagle and an 8 on the 17th, one of the hardest par 4s in championship golf. Level par through 16 holes, Woosnam drove into the right rough and then played the worst looking hook within memory, squirting his ball all the way across the fairway into a stand of trees and deep grass. Then, his line to the green totally blocked, Woosnam tried to save one stroke and lost four, twice hitting shots that moved only a few feet before declaring his ball unplayable and one-putting to save his 8.

Daly began the defence of his championship by birdieing five of the first 11 holes but stumbled in with 70. Greg Norman, saying that for a time he had become bored with golf, shot 71, along with Costantino Rocca, who lost a play-off to Daly at St Andrews. The recent winners of two other important championships played worse. Steve Jones, who surprised everyone by winning the US Open three weeks ear-

John Daly began with 70, after going out in 31.

Hidemichi Tanaka (left) shot 67 and Shigeki Maruyama (right) 68 to provide a strong Japanese presence.

lier, shot 73, and Steve Elkington, the 1995 USPGA champion, shot 75. They would have to improve considerably to survive the 36-hole cut.

While finding Broadhurst at the head of the field wasn't predictable, at the same time it wasn't surprising, for he had a history of low scores. He had shot 63 in the third round of the 1990 Open, at St Andrews, and he won the 1995 French Open over the difficult National Golf Club, in Paris, with another 63. Then, when he had to finish second in the German Open to win a place on the 1991 Ryder Cup team, he came through with a round of 65 and made the team.

At the same time he can go the other way. Even though he won the French Open in 1995, he made 9 on one hole, and the week before the 1996 Open, he took five putts on one of Carnoustie's greens during the Scottish Open.

There were no five-putt greens at Lytham, though, for his putting could hardly have been better. He had only 11 putts on his last 10 holes, and only 23 over the entire 18.

Thirty years old by 1996, with wavy red hair and a ruddy complexion, Broadhurst teed off at 10.29 on Thursday. By then it had become clear that Lytham would indeed give up low scores. It had been put

under attack as soon as play began. Dressed in black shirt, black trousers, a black visor and black-and-white shoes, Malcolm Mackenzie played the first shot of the day, at 7 o'clock in the morning. A 5-foot-8-inch Englishman who had missed the 36-hole cut in seven of the 17 tournaments he had entered, Mackenzie went out in 34, one under par, and followed with birdies on both the 10th, a relatively simple par 4, and the 12th, a tough and demanding par 3. Now he stood at three under par with a series of six consecutive par 4s ahead of him.

Mackenzie was grouped with Arnaud Langenaeken, a 22-year-old Belgian, who was playing almost as well. Langenaeken matched Mackenzie's birdie on the 12th and lagged only one stroke behind. Both men lost strokes over the brutal closing holes, but they had made it clear that Lytham was in trouble.

As they began their last few holes, other, more celebrated golfers were already well into their rounds. Couples and Tanaka stood at four under par, and McCumber, Roberts, Faxon and Lehman stood at three under. By 12.30, Couples and McCumber had completed their rounds in 67, and Faldo and Harrington had shot 68. Tanaka and Faxon stood four under par through the 14th hole; Roberts had birdied three of the four par-3 holes and stood five under

Loren Roberts (67) took 5 on the 18th hole.

Padraig Harrington (68) bogeyed the first.

through the 12th, and O'Meara stood four under through the 13th.

Meantime, Broadhurst had begun making his move. Playing what appeared to be cautious golf, he drove with a two iron on the second, a two iron on the third and another two iron on the fourth, all par-4 holes, and made his figures on each. He had missed the greens of the two par-3 holes, but he still held at level par through the fifth.

By now it had become clear his short game would be his salvation, because he had hit and held only two greens. It wasn't that he missed with wild shots, but his ball persistently rolled off the back.

"It's so fiery out there," Broadhurst explained, "it's not easy to keep the ball on the green." Still, he had saved his scores by one-putting three of the first five greens.

Now Broadhurst began picking up strokes. Reaching the tee of the sixth, the first of the par 5s, he pulled out his driver for the first time, ripped a long shot that curled round the long fairway bunker set in the face of a mound on the left, and bounded 290 yards down the rolling, tumbling fairway. In prime position now, he rifled a five iron from 197 yards to within eight feet of the cup. Another putt fell, and with an eagle 3, Broadhurst suddenly dipped two

under par.

The seventh looked like another opportunity for a birdie, but his eight-iron second ran over the green and he parred, and followed with another par on the eighth as well.

Picking up the pace now, Broadhurst floated a lovely nine iron onto the ninth green and holed from 30 feet for a birdie 2. Out in 32, he stood three under par and had begun a remarkable streak of one-putting nine consecutive greens, four of them for birdies.

He hit a nine iron to three feet on the 10th, at 334 yards the shortest of the par 4s, and then a short pitch to 12 feet on the 11th after laying up with a five-iron second to avoid bunkers on either side of the green. Both putts fell, and now Broadhurst had gone five under par, clearly with a chance to claim the first-round lead.

Now began a run of remarkable saves. He holed from three feet on the 12th, from two feet on the 13th, from 12 feet on the 14th, from four feet on the 15th and from three feet on the 16th, all for pars. He was still five under par with two holes to play. Only Brooks had a chance to catch him now, but Brooks still had all those hard finishing holes ahead of him.

Broadhurst hadn't posted his score yet, either, and he still had the brutal 17th to play, a 467-yard par 4

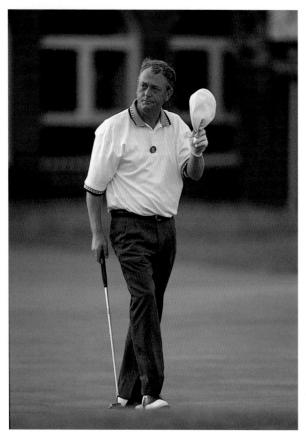

Carl Mason (68) bogeyed three of the last four holes.

Jim Furyk (68) finished with a birdie.

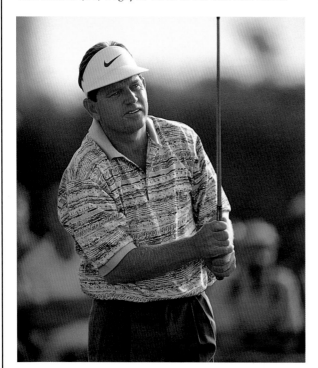

1994 champion Nick Price (68) had an eagle on the sixth.

where 66 contestants took 5s or worse. Taking a deep breath, Broadhurst lashed a long and straight drive and followed with a superb seven iron 30 feet from the cup. Still another putt dropped and Broadhurst slipped six under par with only the home hole left.

A driver that missed all those bunkers, and then a fine eight iron to 15 feet set up still another birdie opening. Strangely, though, the putt missed, and he had his first two-putt green since the eighth hole.

Broadhurst was in with 65, and although he was challenged twice that day, his score held up. After reaching five under par with his birdie on the 11th, Brooks bogeyed the 12th and finished with 67. Very late in the day, Mason, who had tied Broadhurst in the 1988 Open, birdied five holes on the first nine and went out in 31 (he bogeyed the fifth), picked up another birdie at the 10th to reach five under, but then bogeyed three of the last four holes and shot 68.

Daly played the first nine in 31 as well, then birdied the 11th by reaching the green not with a wedge this time but with his famous zero iron, a club with 10 degrees of loft. That was his last glowing moment. He bunkered his tee shot to the 12th and

28

Craig Stadler (71) and Ernie Els (68) relaxed as they waited their turn on the 17th tee.

bogeyed. He pulled his tee shot against a grandstand on the 13th, played a poor pitch, and three-putted from 40 feet. He missed the green at the 16th, drove into a bunker at the 17th, and did well to bogey both holes. After a glorious start, he had come back in 39 and shot 70, one under par. While he said he felt he still had a chance, he fell steadily behind.

Broadhurst, of course, was euphoric.

"It's tremendous," he said. "Everyone thinks of leading the Open, and I'm no exception. I would definitely put this among the best rounds I've ever played, but I probably didn't play as well as I can. It was difficult to keep the ball on the fairways and greens. It was very bouncy; you have to think your way round and try not to make any mistakes. The main thing is to get the ball on the fairway. If you miss, you're not going to get it on the green."

Asked if he thought he could win, Broadhurst said: "I think I'm good enough to win; I'm pretty confident I can stay up there, but whether it happens is another thing. I'll just go out and shoot the best score I can.

"I play very late tomorrow. I'm sure I will be extremely nervous."

Nick Faldo (68) went three under on the second nine.

# FIRST ROUND RESULTS

| HOLE | 1 | 2 | 3 | 4 | 5 | 6 | 7 | 8 | 9 | 10 | 11 | 12 | 13 | 14 | 15 | 16 | 17 | 18 | |
|---|---|---|---|---|---|---|---|---|---|---|---|---|---|---|---|---|---|---|---|
| PAR | 3 | 4 | 4 | 4 | 3 | 5 | 5 | 4 | 3 | 4 | 5 | 3 | 4 | 4 | 4 | 4 | 4 | 4 | TOTAL |
| Paul Broadhurst | 3 | 4 | 4 | 4 | 3 | 3 | 5 | 4 | 2 | 3 | 4 | 3 | 4 | 4 | 4 | 4 | 3 | 4 | 65 |
| Fred Couples | 3 | 4 | 4 | 3 | 2 | 5 | 4 | 4 | 3 | 3 | 4 | 3 | 5 | 4 | 4 | 4 | 4 | 4 | 67 |
| Mark McCumber | 3 | 4 | 5 | 3 | 2 | 4 | 4 | 4 | 3 | 4 | 5 | 3 | 3 | 4 | 5 | 4 | 3 | 4 | 67 |
| Hidemichi Tanaka | 3 | 3 | 4 | 4 | 3 | 4 | 5 | 3 | 2 | 4 | 5 | 3 | 4 | 4 | 4 | 4 | 4 | 4 | 67 |
| Brad Faxon | 3 | 4 | 4 | 4 | 2 | 4 | 5 | 4 | 2 | 4 | 5 | 3 | 3 | 4 | 4 | 4 | 4 | 4 | 67 |
| Mark O'Meara | 2 | 5 | 4 | 4 | 2 | 4 | 4 | 4 | 3 | 4 | 5 | 3 | 3 | 4 | 4 | 4 | 3 | 5 | 67 |
| Tom Lehman | 3 | 4 | 4 | 3 | 2 | 4 | 5 | 4 | 3 | 4 | 5 | 3 | 6 | 3 | 4 | 3 | 3 | 4 | 67 |
| Loren Roberts | 2 | 4 | 4 | 3 | 2 | 5 | 4 | 5 | 3 | 3 | 5 | 2 | 4 | 4 | 5 | 4 | 3 | 5 | 67 |
| Mark Brooks | 3 | 4 | 4 | 3 | 4 | 4 | 3 | 4 | 3 | 3 | 4 | 4 | 3 | 4 | 5 | 4 | 4 | 4 | 67 |
| Nick Faldo | 4 | 4 | 4 | 4 | 3 | 4 | 5 | 4 | 3 | 4 | 4 | 3 | 4 | 4 | 3 | 4 | 4 | 3 | 68 |
| Padraig Harrington | 4 | 4 | 4 | 4 | 3 | 5 | 4 | 4 | 3 | 4 | 4 | 2 | 4 | 4 | 4 | 3 | 4 | 4 | 68 |
| Shigeki Maruyama | 3 | 4 | 4 | 4 | 3 | 3 | 4 | 4 | 3 | 4 | 5 | 3 | 3 | 4 | 6 | 3 | 4 | 4 | 68 |
| Jim Furyk | 3 | 4 | 4 | 4 | 3 | 4 | 5 | 4 | 3 | 3 | 4 | 4 | 5 | 3 | 4 | 4 | 3 | 3 | 68 |
| Ernie Els | 3 | 4 | 4 | 4 | 3 | 4 | 5 | 3 | 3 | 4 | 5 | 3 | 4 | 4 | 3 | 3 | 4 | 5 | 68 |
| Nick Price | 3 | 4 | 4 | 5 | 3 | 3 | 4 | 4 | 2 | 4 | 5 | 3 | 3 | 3 | 5 | 4 | 5 | 5 | 68 |
| Carl Mason | 2 | 3 | 4 | 3 | 4 | 4 | 4 | 4 | 3 | 3 | 5 | 3 | 4 | 4 | 5 | 3 | 5 | 5 | 68 |
| Klas Eriksson | 4 | 4 | 3 | 5 | 3 | 4 | 4 | 3 | 2 | 4 | 5 | 4 | 4 | 4 | 4 | 3 | 4 | 4 | 68 |

# HOLE SUMMARY

| HOLE | PAR | EAGLES | BIRDIES | PARS | BOGEYS | HIGHER | RANK | AVERAGE |
|---|---|---|---|---|---|---|---|---|
| 1 | 3 | 0 | 16 | 112 | 24 | 4 | 9 | 3.10 |
| 2 | 4 | 0 | 13 | 112 | 27 | 4 | 8 | 4.14 |
| 3 | 4 | 0 | 13 | 96 | 38 | 9 | 3 | 4.29 |
| 4 | 4 | 0 | 21 | 112 | 23 | 0 | 12 | 4.01 |
| 5 | 3 | 0 | 12 | 112 | 31 | 1 | 7 | 3.13 |
| 6 | 5 | 14 | 66 | 63 | 13 | 0 | 18 | 4.48 |
| 7 | 5 | 7 | 63 | 75 | 9 | 2 | 17 | 4.59 |
| 8 | 4 | 0 | 11 | 105 | 34 | 6 | 6 | 4.23 |
| 9 | 3 | 0 | 11 | 125 | 19 | 1 | 11 | 3.06 |
| OUT | 35 | 21 | 226 | 912 | 218 | 27 | | 35.03 |
| 10 | 4 | 0 | 33 | 108 | 14 | 1 | 15 | 3.89 |
| 11 | 5 | 0 | 58 | 74 | 19 | 5 | 16 | 4.81 |
| 12 | 3 | 0 | 12 | 100 | 43 | 1 | 4 | 3.21 |
| 13 | 4 | 1 | 28 | 103 | 22 | 2 | 14 | 3.97 |
| 14 | 4 | 0 | 15 | 111 | 26 | 4 | 10 | 4.12 |
| 15 | 4 | 0 | 6 | 84 | 54 | 12 | 1 | 4.47 |
| 16 | 4 | 1 | 25 | 103 | 25 | 2 | 12 | 4.01 |
| 17 | 4 | 0 | 13 | 77 | 53 | 13 | 2 | 4.45 |
| 18 | 4 | 0 | 11 | 103 | 33 | 9 | 5 | 4.26 |
| IN | 36 | 2 | 201 | 863 | 289 | 49 | | 37.19 |
| TOTAL | 71 | 23 | 427 | 1775 | 507 | 76 | | 72.22 |

| | | | |
|---|---|---|---|
| Players Below Par | 42 | | |
| Players At Par | 20 | | |
| Players Above Par | 94 | | |

## WEATHER

Dry and sunny.
Wind light and variable.

## LOW SCORES

| Low First Nine | John Daly | 31 |
|---|---|---|
| | Carl Mason | 31 |
| | Hidemichi Tanaka | 31 |
| Low Second Nine | Paul Broadhurst | 33 |
| | Nick Faldo | 33 |
| | Padraig Harrington | 33 |
| Low Round | Paul Broadhurst | 65 |

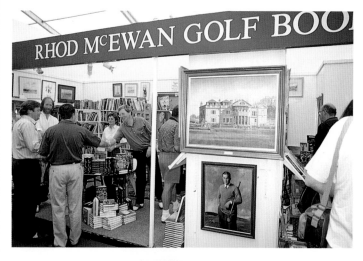

The Exhibition Tent offered a variety of shops and activities.

"I still remember most of the shots I played in the last few holes in 1979 and 1988," Seve Ballesteros said. "They are great memories, so I am very happy to be here and very grateful to this place."

# COMMENTARY

# 'WELCOME HOME, SEVE'

## BY MICHAEL WILLIAMS

Such has been the tread of generations of golfers that the grey front step that leads into the clubhouse at Royal Lytham and St Annes has become concave, but so off centre that it would seem everybody leads with their right foot. Beyond it is the swivel door, beyond that the square, welcoming entrance hall, an old-fashioned stove spreading warmth in winter, window seats to the right, the porter's cubbyhole to the left, a broad staircase doubling back on itself and leading to an upstairs landing on the walls of which are photographs of the past captains.

It is a front step that has borne the hopes and aspirations of thousands of golfers when first they arrive, a step that has sent a tiny minority away in exultation and countless numbers in disappointment.

No doubt Severiano Ballesteros also "led with his right" when first in this summer of 1996 he went through the swivel door, peeling away half left to the locker room where, turning sharp right, he was directed to the last row, which was reserved for past champions.

Pinned to the front of his locker, the first on the left, he found a note, hand-written, on the club's notepaper. It read: "Welcome home, Seve, we all want you to win again. Good luck, from the Members." A superstitious man, Ballesteros vowed there and then not to take it down. To do so might deny him the luck he knew he would need. Each day it would remind him how many were wishing him well on a golf course where luck had already visited him twice.

This is not to be disparaging. In the aftermath of his many victories all over the world across the last 20 years, Ballesteros has unfailingly emphasised "I was very lucky." Winners always are. However high the level of vision, ball control, the mastery of shot, there is always the fortunate bounce somewhere along the line, the putt that drops when, on another day, it would have missed. Twice, therefore, Ballesteros had

enjoyed the run of the ball at Royal Lytham. It was here in 1979 that at the age of 22 he had won his first Open; here again in 1988 that he had won his third. Another eight years on and here he was again, his wardrobe already fixed for Sunday, superstition still uppermost.

In 1979 he had worn a dark blue pullover, slacks to match. His shirt was white and so were his shoes. It was the same in 1988. "The only thing that has changed is that I am nine years older," he said in the aftermath of his thrilling final round of 65, which only just fended off the bravest of challenges from Nick Price. That was vintage Ballesteros, his finest hour, given the circumstances. As the 1996 championship drew ever closer, Ballesteros often let his mind wander back to that day. "Only once or twice in a lifetime a man gets to play that well," he reflected. "I knew I had reached some sort of peak and it was a round of golf I will remember for the rest of my life."

But now another eight years had passed. Ballesteros was 39 and seemingly in the slowly lengthening shadows of his career, no longer the player he was; even he has been forced to acknowledge that. In the depths of winter I had visited him at the golf club where he grew up, Pedrena, in northern Spain. It was February and a great wind blew in off the Bay of Biscay, and Ballesteros was coming to the end of a six-month break from tournament golf. The last time he had played had been in September of the previous year in the Ryder Cup at Oak Hill, a match he more than anyone had helped to revive since his first appearance in 1979 when the continental players were allowed in to stiffen the British backbone.

His contribution at Oak Hill, other than his inspiring presence, had been minimal. Significantly, Bernard Gallacher, the captain, had not even played him in the opening series of foursomes. His only point had come in a fourball with David Gilford, who

Ballesteros started with 74, and would miss the cut.

largely carried a man who previously could have carried anyone.

In the singles he had played top but he was no match for Tom Lehman who, though no one knew it at the time, would succeed Ballesteros as an Open champion at Royal Lytham. Ballesteros could not hit a fairway for love nor money. He was worn out. For 20 years and more he had been at the top of the golfing tree, three Opens, two US Masters and altogether 72 tournament victories world-wide. And always there were the interviews, day after day, win, lose or draw.

Now, as a new season for him approached, he boasted of the weight he had lost, the weights he had lifted, the miles he had cycled, up hill and down dale. But when I asked him whether he really had another major championship left in him, he was more cautious. "Definitely my confidence is getting lower," he said. "But I am fighting. This game is very unpredictable. I have seen so many things over the years, nothing surprises me any more."

Shortly afterwards Ballesteros was confirmed as captain of the European Ryder Cup team for the 1997 match at Valderrama on Spain's Costa del Sol, a logical choice for a match that had never before been held outside Great Britain. Logically, he should also be the non-playing captain because the duties are now too great to cope with playing as well. There would be too great a danger of his "taking his eye off the ball."

But it is a point Ballesteros refuses to concede. He admits "it would be difficult — but possible." Nor is he alone in that. Tom Watson and Lanny Wadkins, two recent American captains, thought the same and so does Tom Kite, Ballesteros' opposite number at Valderrama. But the fact remains that there has not been a playing captain on either side since Arnold Palmer in 1963.

Ballesteros spent the week immediately before this Open Championship back at his home in Pedrena, isolating himself from the world just as he had done in the winter when he enjoyed the simpler things in life, like taking the children to school, spending time with friends, reading the paper in a coffee bar and then feeling uncomfortable as he watched others going to work.

These had been pleasures he had missed; 20 years had flashed by and suddenly the children were growing up and he realised the price paid for fame and fortune. But now it was July again, the Open again and Lytham again and Ballesteros was back. He was soon called to the interview tent to face an expectant media. "It's been a long time," he said, "but I still remember most of the shots I played in the last few holes in 1979 and 1988. They are great memories, so I am very happy to be here and very grateful to this place.

"In 1979 I remember very well the birdie I made at the 13th from the right side of the green, and obviously the famous birdie on the 16th from the car park, and two putts from the front part of the green at the 18th," Ballesteros said. "From 1988 I remember very well the birdie I also made at the 13th, also the birdie at the 16th from the middle of the fairway this time, and the good chip at the 18th. I watched it a couple of times last week on video and I think, one of these days it is going to go in. I tried it today but it didn't go in because the hole was not there!"

Ballesteros remembered, too, his second round in 1979 when, beginning at the 14th, he finished 3, 3, 4, 3, 3, playing with Lee Trevino. That was four birdies over the hardest stretch of the golf course. But that was also 17 years ago when he hardly seemed more than a boy, one still struggling with what to him was a foreign tongue, though at least he did not need an interpreter, as he had done at Royal Birkdale in 1976 when runner-up with Jack Nicklaus to Johnny Miller.

"When I watch the films of my Opens, I see if I can pick up anything that I am not doing now," he said. "I'm just sad that I can't be youthful forever but no one can do that, everyone is going to die, that is the only truth in life. You can't do anything about it. You just have to take it."

He had to take, too, what was already a disappointing season. On the European circuit he had played 10 tournaments, missed the cut four times and not had a single top-10 finish. In the US Masters at Augusta he had made all four rounds but, tellingly, he decided not to try and qualify for the US Open. Sadly, one has to say that it was the right decision. Oakland Hills was no place for Ballesteros in his current form. Yet there still was the air of bravado about him. "My last few tournaments in Europe do not show the way I have been playing," he insisted. "I feel I waste two or three shots every round that I shouldn't. My game is not 100 per cent but it is not as bad as some people may think. I believe that."

So did others. As he practised, his eye caught a banner hanging from the same house it had done in 1988 on the other side of the railway flanking the second hole. Translated from Spanish it read: "Seve please win again." The members at Royal Lytham were not the only ones on his side.

But dreams were to perish. Ballesteros was out early on Thursday and no one complains about that. He was cheered to every green but, like his golf, it was more in hope than expectation. "I drove like a soldier," he described it. "Left, right, left, right and when you do that you are not sure what you are doing wrong." He dropped his first stroke at the third, another at the sixth. Two mighty woods got him home in two at the seventh and he had his first birdie; but the lengthened eighth cost him a shot and he was out in 37.

Ballesteros got back to one over par with a 20-foot putt for a 4 at the 11th, only then to take 5s at the 13th and 15th. His "old friend," the 16th, produced a birdie, but a 74, nine strokes behind Paul Broadhurst and scores of others, indicated that he might

Waving as he departed, Ballesteros finished with 78.

soon be on his way home again.

He was. On the Friday he took 78 and missed the cut. All he could take home with him was the sympathy of the crowds. "They were very special," he said. "On every hole, every tee, every green, fantastic. But it was not enough for me to play better.

"I did not bring my game with me. For the first six holes today I played well, and then it went. I try my best but it just did not happen and everything went wrong. I still love this place and when the Open comes back to Lytham I will be back. I don't know what it will need to get my game back but I still think I can get it back. I am having a tough time but I will always do the best I can, be patient and keep working."

As he talked, Ballesteros glanced up at the big leaderboard. And there was the name of Jack Nicklaus with rounds of 69, 66 and sharing second place. "He is 56 and I am 39," he told himself. "There is plenty of time yet." But Nicklaus is Nicklaus and Ballesteros is Ballesteros. Both have won three Open Championships. In every other respect they are very different.

"To be leading the Open at this stage is something you dream about," Paul McGinley said. "I never got ahead of myself. I was always in the present. I never got too excited. I kept things in perspective."

# McGINLEY RAISES IRISH HOPES

## BY ROBERT SOMMERS

Something about Royal Lytham and St Annes seems to renew if not the sinew then the spirit of those who have passed the shady side of 50. In Lytham's first Open, back in 1926, J.H. Taylor shot 304 and tied for 11th place, 13 strokes behind Bobby Jones. Taylor was aged 55 at the time. Thirty-two years later Gene Sarazen shot 288, tied Bobby Locke and Max Faulkner for 16th place, and finished 10 strokes behind Peter Thomson, who won his fourth Open. Sarazen was aged 56.

One round does not make a championship, but when Jack Nicklaus cruised round Lytham in 66 early in the second round, it thrust him into second place, one stroke behind Paul McGinley, a short, broad-shouldered Irishman, who had shot 65 early in the day and held first place. Jack was aged 56 as well; his sparkling round drove the gallery nearly into a frenzy and stirred hope he might hold on for two more days and reprise his wonderful victory in the US Masters 10 years earlier. Realistically they understood, though, that this was more likely a moment similar to Ben Hogan's marvellous 66 in the second round of the 1967 US Masters, when Hogan was aged 54.

Late in the afternoon, Tom Lehman shot a second 67 and tied McGinley at 134. With 135, Nicklaus ended the day tied with Ernie Els and Peter Hedblom, a blond-haired, 26-year-old Swede struggling to make his way on the PGA European Tour. Hedblom as well as McGinley had shot 65, the best scores of the day. Meantime, Paul Broadhurst, the first-round leader, played an erratic round of 72 and slipped into a tie for 13th place, at 137. With a second consecutive 68, Nick Faldo was tied with six others at 136, only two strokes off the lead, along with Corey Pavin, Loren Roberts, Mark O'Meara, Vijay Singh, Padraig Harrington and Mark McCumber.

Fred Couples and Mark Brooks, who had opened with 67s, slipped into a tie with Broadhurst after

shooting 70s. Hidemichi Tanaka shot 71 and 138, and Brad Faxon shot 73 and 140. Couples and Brooks would continue to challenge the leaders but the others would fall behind.

Once again the temperature climbed into the mid-20s Celsius (high 70s and low 80s Fahrenheit), causing the gallery to leave their rainsuits and sweaters in their homes or hotels. Some wore shorts and some men took off their shirts and sunned themselves in chairs in the tented village or propped against the steel rods that held the gallery ropes. Balls that carried into the paths the gallery had worn bare often raised puffs of dust, and those that actually hit the fairways ran incredible distances. It was on this day that Lehman pounded a 350-yard drive on the seventh, and followed with a 200-yard eight iron that bounded and rolled onto the green.

The greens had turned as hard as rocks; it was common for players to have trouble finding their pitch marks, and consequently they played run-up shots, especially on the longer holes. Nevertheless, the field scored even better than in the first round. Where 42 men broke par on Thursday, 57 shot under 71 on Friday, and where 17 players had scored under 69 on Thursday, 23 shot 68 or better on Friday.

McGinley and Hedblom had the lowest scores, of course, but in addition to Nicklaus, 66s were shot by Corey Pavin, Tom Kite and Eldrick (Tiger) Woods, the US Amateur champion. Those having 67s were Lehman, Els, Singh, David Gilford, David Duval, David Feherty and Alexander Cejka. Woods' score matched Frank Stranahan's 66 at Troon in 1950 as the lowest ever shot by an amateur in the Open.

By the time Broadhurst teed off at 3.15, he knew what he would have to do to hold his place, for McGinley had finished long before then with one of the more sensational first nines of recent memory. Climaxed by a hole-in-one on the ninth, he went out

Tom Lehman (134) returned a second 67.

Peter Hedblom (135) birdied two of the last three for 65.

in 29, the ninth 29 in Open history and the fifth at Royal Lytham. The record, though, stands at 28, shot by Denis Durnian at Royal Birkdale in 1983.

Teeing off at 7.22, McGinley attacked from the start, rifling a four iron 12 feet from the cup and birdieing the first hole. After holing a saving six-footer on the second, he holed again from six feet after a good seven iron to the fourth and went two under par.

There was a missed opportunity on the sixth, where McGinley missed the green with his second and settled for par on a hole that half the field birdied that day (76 birdies, two eagles), but he did birdie the seventh, holing from 15 feet, and followed with another at the eighth after a seven-iron approach to three feet. Then he scored his hole-in-one, the sixth of his career, his fourth as a professional, and his second in the Open. He had holed-in-one on Muirfield's seventh during the 1992 championship.

Situated at the very end of the Royal Lytham property, close by the Woodlands Road Club where members watch the Open from their porch, the ninth measures 164 yards from a high tee to an undulating green nearly ringed by deep, menacing bunkers. McGinley played a seven iron that drew in nicely, hit about eight feet short of the cup, took the backspin, and wedged between the flagstick and the rim of the cup. He had played his last three holes in four under par.

His second nine wasn't nearly so gripping. He struggled with the 11th and failed to birdie, then saved par from a bunker on the 12th after what he described as his worst swing of the day. His recovery hit the flagstick and he holed from three feet. He fell to seven under par by playing a wedge to three feet on the 14th, a hole that measures 445 yards, then gave that stroke away by bogeying the 15th, 463 yards of terror. Playing a six iron for his second, he had expected his ball to bounce toward the green, but it hit a soft spot, pulled up short, and he played an indifferent chip. He made up for it by birdieing the 17th with a perfectly gauged four iron to 25 feet.

Seven under now, he needed one more par 4 to shoot 64 and break the course record. Instead, he drove into the rough on the 18th, and from a flier lie

With a par on the 18th, Jack Nicklaus (135) was in with 66, one stroke off the lead.

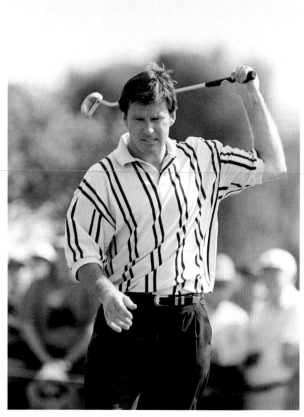

Nick Faldo (136) bogeyed only the 12th.

Ernie Els (135) birdied the 18th for 67.

ran his ball over the back of the green, then missed his putt from four feet.

Still, he had played the round of his life, and he was indeed fortunate to have played in the Open at all. He was among those who had fought the winds at Carnoustie the previous week, shot 307, then raced down to Lytham to meet a 7.25 starting time in the next day's qualifying round. Somehow his swing returned to normal and he shot 66 in the first round and qualified easily. It was quite a change from Carnoustie, where he never shot lower than 75 and finished 19 strokes over par.

Speaking of his round later, McGinley said he tried not to get ahead of himself and keep everything in perspective.

This was his fourth Open, his first time making the cut. Until this year he had played only one round under 70 in the Open, a 69 in the second round at Muirfield, where he made the hole-in-one, and now he had shot 69 and 65. A product of the Irish junior programme that also produced such first-class players as Darren Clarke, who lurked four strokes behind McGinley at 138, Ronan Rafferty, Philip

Padraig Harrington (136) posted 68 with brilliant play around the greens.

Walton, Des Smyth and the amateur Garth McGimpsey, McGinley had gone to the United States and played golf at International University in San Diego.

Returning home, he played on the 1991 Walker Cup team along with Padraig Harrington, whose two 68s placed him just two strokes behind the leaders.

Harrington had played the first two rounds with Fred Couples and Mark McCumber. They made an interesting group to watch; not only were they playing well, both Couples and especially McCumber constantly encouraged Harrington. When he birdied the 12th by holing a long putt, McCumber applauded along with the gallery. Then, when he holed from a bunker on the 18th, McCumber walked over to him and they exchanged high-fives.

Harrington wrung about as much out of his round as he could, but McCumber's might have been better. On the other hand, he was fortunate to have played at all. Along with Curtis Strange and Jay Haas, he had played at Williamsburg, Virginia, the previous week, then boarded a private aeroplane for

Corey Pavin (136) was 11 strokes ahead of Gary Player.

Mark McCumber (136) shot 69 after he bogeyed four of the last six holes.

Mark Brooks (137) finished with nine 4s and 70.

a flight to Newark, New Jersey, Sunday night. Approaching Newark, the aeroplane turned back to Virginia because of stormy weather. They tried again the next day, but they were diverted to Long Island, New York, where they had a scary landing. McCumber said he saw both the pilot and co-pilot struggling with the controls as they landed in a strong crosswind.

From the terminal they took a cab and raced to JFK International Airport, hoping to catch a flight around 6 o'clock, missed that flight by five minutes, and took another an hour later. They didn't reach the golf course until 4.30 Tuesday afternoon. Then Strange broke a toe after he arrived.

McCumber admitted they thought of withdrawing, but they brushed the thought aside. McCumber, of course, was playing best; Haas had shot 142 and Strange 143, just making the 36-hole cut.

His 45th birthday barely two months away, McCumber realised his chances of winning were running out, but he hadn't dismissed the possibility. "I'll always come over to play if I'm exempt from qualifying," he said. "Of course if I were to win, I would be exempt for years, wouldn't I?"

Off to a quick start, McCumber rushed to the turn

Mark O'Meara (136) went out in 31 and shot 69.

in 32 with three birdies, then picked up two more on the 11th and the 12th, a very difficult par 3 of 198 yards that gave up only 11 birdies all day, fewer than any other hole except, strangely, the third, a par 4 of 457 yards, which also had 11. McCumber stood five under par then, but he could go no further.

Lytham finishes with six consecutive par 4s, some of them absolutely terrifying, pocked with steep-faced fairway bunkers where sod is laid like bricks, one layer atop another, so deep a man can disappear from sight. The holes range in distance from the 342-yard 13th, which does give up birdies, to the 467-yard 17th, the hole Bobby Jones had made famous in 1926. McCumber bogeyed both the 13th and the 14th, made his par on the 15th, and closed out his round with bogeys on the 17th and 18th.

Vijay Singh (136) birdied the 18th for 67.

His approach to the 18th frightened a year off the lives of Lytham members who cowered inside their red brick clubhouse as McCumber's ball, played from a fluffy lie in the rough, bounded over the green, banged off the wall of the clubhouse, and nearly rebounded onto the green. "For a moment I thought I was flying my ball right through the window into somebody's beer," McCumber quipped.

From there he played a wobbly chip to about six or eight feet and missed the putt. Instead of the 66 or 67 he might have shot, he finished with 69, still quite good enough to remain close to the leaders.

The feeling persisted, though, that Lehman was the bigger threat, principally because he had come so close to winning important tournaments in the past. After years of struggling on mini-tours, Lehman, who is aged 37 now, had burst into prominence by nearly winning the 1994 US Masters. He shot 72 in the last round, his worst score of the tournament, and finished two strokes behind Jose Maria Olazabal.

He went into the last round of the 1995 US Open tied for the lead with Greg Norman and once again

Loren Roberts (136) birdied the 18th for 69.

Tiger Woods (141) shot 66 to equal Frank Stranahan's record score for an amateur, set 46 years ago.

Other amateur stars missed the cut, including 16-year-old Sergio Garcia (left) and Amateur champion Warren Bladon (right).

shot his worst score, closing with 74, and falling to third behind Corey Pavin and Norman. Three weeks before the 1996 Open he bogeyed the 18th hole at Oakland Hills and lost the US Open to Steve Jones by one stroke. It was clear that Tom Lehman must be dealt with in major championships.

He was introduced to the Open at Sandwich in 1993, opened with respectable rounds of 69 and 71, and eventually tied for 59th place. The following year he improved to a tie for 24th, but skipped the 1995 championship to be at home for the birth of his son.

Asked what the Open means to him, Lehman said it used to be good entertainment on television, "all those pot bunkers and crazy bounces. I realise now that if you're serious about being a great player, you've got to come here."

He carefully prepared this year, and after two rounds seemed incapable of shooting anything other than 67. Off to a rough start when he missed the first green and bogeyed, Lehman won the stroke back by holing from 25 feet on the second, and then birdied both those vulnerable par 5s. Out in 33, he played

steadily through the second nine, picking up one birdie on the 13th, which was not unexpected, and another on the 17th, which was, for the 17th played as the third hardest hole of the day. Lehman played a three wood into good position, then lofted a wedge that hit the green and braked within 12 feet of the cup. He had a slight struggle with the home hole, but holed a six-footer for the par 4 and a second nine of 34.

With all the low scoring, the 36-hole cut fell at 143, one stroke above par, and it caught a number of prominent players. Principally among them was Colin Montgomerie, who played the last nine in 39, with a double bogey on the 13th, when he needed 35 to survive. With 147 he had his fourth missed cut in five years, prompting him to say: "I save my worst golf of the year for the third week in July."

Sam Torrance went out with 144, one too many. Steve Elkington prepared to defend his USPGA Championship by shooting 145. Less than a month after winning the US Open, Steve Jones left town with 146, the same score as Davis Love III, who played the last four holes in four over par with two

Fred Couples (137) shot 70 despite five bogeys.

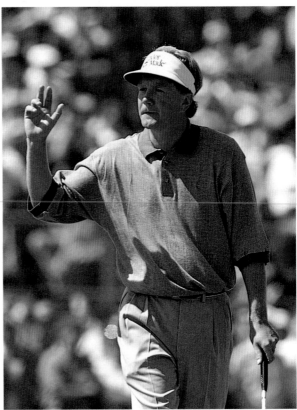

Paul Broadhurst (137) shot 72 with an eagle.

double bogeys, one bogey and a birdie on the 17th. Ian Woosnam shot 147; Paul Azinger and Lee Janzen shot 151, and while the huge gallery bordering the 18th cheered, Seve Ballesteros lost three strokes on the last two holes and left with 152.

Unable to raise his club beyond hip-high, Bernhard Langer had withdrawn earlier in the day with an injury to his left shoulder; and both Michael Campbell, who played so well at St Andrews a year earlier, and Des Smyth were disqualified. Campbell's marker hadn't noticed him taking penalty drops on the 10th and 13th; Campbell didn't check the scores and was judged guilty of signing for a score lower than he actually shot.

Then there was Ian Baker-Finch, the 1991 champion, who has evidently forgotten how to play. After opening with 78, Baker-Finch played the last five holes in six over par, shot 84, and with 162 finished dead last among those who actually turned in scores. His last drive may have indicated the extent of his miseries. It shot off dead right, missed the fairway, missed the rough, and bounded to the fringes of the tented village. It was found next to the Bollinger tent by a woman wearing high heels and sipping a glass of champagne.

Michael Campbell was disqualified with an incorrect card.

Davis Love III (146) missed the 36-hole cut.

Phil Mickelson (143) was on the cut-off score.

Greg Norman (139) was in contention after a 68.

# SECOND ROUND RESULTS

| HOLE | 1 | 2 | 3 | 4 | 5 | 6 | 7 | 8 | 9 | 10 | 11 | 12 | 13 | 14 | 15 | 16 | 17 | 18 | |
|---|---|---|---|---|---|---|---|---|---|---|---|---|---|---|---|---|---|---|---|
| PAR | 3 | 4 | 4 | 4 | 3 | 5 | 5 | 4 | 3 | 4 | 5 | 3 | 4 | 4 | 4 | 4 | 4 | 4 | TOTAL |
| Paul McGinley | 2 | 4 | 4 | 3 | 3 | 5 | 4 | 3 | 1 | 4 | 5 | 3 | 4 | 3 | 5 | 4 | 3 | 5 | 65-134 |
| Tom Lehman | 4 | 3 | 4 | 4 | 3 | 4 | 4 | 4 | 3 | 4 | 5 | 3 | 3 | 4 | 4 | 4 | 3 | 4 | 67-134 |
| Jack Nicklaus | 2 | 4 | 4 | 4 | 3 | 5 | 4 | 4 | 2 | 3 | 5 | 3 | 4 | 3 | 4 | 4 | 4 | 4 | 66-135 |
| Peter Hedblom | 4 | 3 | 4 | 5 | 3 | 4 | 4 | 4 | 3 | 3 | 4 | 3 | 4 | 3 | 4 | 3 | 3 | 4 | 65-135 |
| Ernie Els | 4 | 3 | 4 | 4 | 3 | 5 | 3 | 4 | 3 | 3 | 5 | 3 | 4 | 3 | 5 | 4 | 4 | 3 | 67-135 |
| Vijay Singh | 3 | 4 | 5 | 3 | 3 | 5 | 4 | 3 | 3 | 4 | 4 | 3 | 4 | 4 | 4 | 3 | 5 | 3 | 67-136 |
| Corey Pavin | 2 | 4 | 5 | 4 | 3 | 4 | 5 | 4 | 2 | 4 | 4 | 4 | 3 | 3 | 4 | 3 | 4 | 4 | 66-136 |
| Nick Faldo | 3 | 4 | 4 | 3 | 3 | 5 | 4 | 4 | 3 | 3 | 5 | 4 | 4 | 4 | 4 | 3 | 4 | 4 | 68-136 |
| Mark McCumber | 3 | 3 | 4 | 4 | 2 | 4 | 5 | 4 | 3 | 4 | 4 | 2 | 5 | 5 | 4 | 3 | 5 | 5 | 69-136 |
| Padraig Harrington | 3 | 4 | 4 | 4 | 3 | 4 | 5 | 5 | 2 | 4 | 5 | 2 | 5 | 4 | 4 | 4 | 3 | 3 | 68-136 |
| Mark O'Meara | 3 | 4 | 3 | 4 | 3 | 4 | 4 | 3 | 3 | 4 | 5 | 3 | 5 | 4 | 4 | 4 | 4 | 5 | 69-136 |
| Loren Roberts | 3 | 4 | 4 | 4 | 3 | 4 | 4 | 5 | 3 | 4 | 5 | 3 | 4 | 4 | 4 | 3 | 4 | 3 | 69-136 |
| Mark Brooks | 4 | 4 | 4 | 4 | 3 | 4 | 5 | 3 | 3 | 4 | 4 | 4 | 4 | 4 | 4 | 4 | 4 | 4 | 70-137 |
| Fred Couples | 3 | 5 | 4 | 5 | 4 | 4 | 3 | 3 | 3 | 3 | 5 | 3 | 3 | 4 | 5 | 4 | 5 | 4 | 70-137 |
| Paul Broadhurst | 3 | 4 | 3 | 5 | 3 | 5 | 4 | 5 | 4 | 6 | 3 | 3 | 4 | 5 | 4 | 3 | 4 | 4 | 72-137 |

# HOLE SUMMARY

| HOLE | PAR | EAGLES | BIRDIES | PARS | BOGEYS | HIGHER | RANK | AVERAGE |
|---|---|---|---|---|---|---|---|---|
| 1 | 3 | 0 | 18 | 100 | 34 | 3 | 9 | 3.14 |
| 2 | 4 | 0 | 12 | 105 | 35 | 3 | 7 | 4.19 |
| 3 | 4 | 0 | 11 | 90 | 48 | 6 | 4 | 4.32 |
| 4 | 4 | 0 | 27 | 104 | 23 | 1 | 12 | 3.99 |
| 5 | 3 | 0 | 12 | 92 | 48 | 3 | 1 | 3.27 |
| 6 | 5 | 2 | 76 | 65 | 10 | 2 | 18 | 4.57 |
| 7 | 5 | 6 | 70 | 65 | 11 | 3 | 17 | 4.59 |
| 8 | 4 | 0 | 21 | 89 | 40 | 5 | 7 | 4.19 |
| 9 | 3 | 1 | 36 | 96 | 20 | 2 | 14 | 2.91 |
| OUT | 35 | 9 | 283 | 806 | 269 | 28 | | 35.17 |
| 10 | 4 | 0 | 37 | 94 | 23 | 1 | 13 | 3.92 |
| 11 | 5 | 3 | 57 | 71 | 21 | 3 | 16 | 4.77 |
| 12 | 3 | 0 | 11 | 96 | 44 | 4 | 2 | 3.26 |
| 13 | 4 | 0 | 33 | 96 | 19 | 7 | 11 | 4.00 |
| 14 | 4 | 0 | 21 | 112 | 21 | 1 | 10 | 4.01 |
| 15 | 4 | 0 | 13 | 102 | 34 | 6 | 5 | 4.21 |
| 16 | 4 | 0 | 42 | 93 | 18 | 2 | 15 | 3.87 |
| 17 | 4 | 0 | 16 | 86 | 41 | 12 | 3 | 4.34 |
| 18 | 4 | 0 | 21 | 88 | 41 | 5 | 6 | 4.20 |
| IN | 36 | 3 | 251 | 838 | 262 | 41 | | 36.58 |
| TOTAL | 71 | 12 | 534 | 1644 | 531 | 69 | | 71.75 |

| Players Below Par | 57 |
|---|---|
| Players At Par | 14 |
| Players Above Par | 84 |

## LOW SCORES

| Low First Nine | Paul McGinley | 29 |
|---|---|---|
| Low Second Nine | Peter Hedblom | 31 |
| | Tom Kite | 31 |
| Low Round | Peter Hedblom | 65 |
| | Paul McGinley | 65 |

## WEATHER

Dry and sunny.
A light wind swinging south to north-west.

Coverage of the Open Championship included the international Press, photographers, television and radio personnel.

Jack Nicklaus now has played on the final day of the Open Championship 31 times — one more than J.H. Taylor.

## COMMENTARY

# NICKLAUS HAS FUN AGAIN

### BY ANDREW FARRELL

It was a day of ovations. For two men it was a feeling they knew well; maybe even this was why they played the game. It may not have been Sunday evening, with victory in hand and with the spine-tingling thrill of walking up the 18th hole at Royal Lytham and St Annes in the knowledge that a century-old silver claret jug was the prize. No, this was Friday, only the second day of the 125th Open Championship. The grandstands were not quite filled to overflowing, as they would be in two days' time, but the warmth of the receptions that awaited Jack Nicklaus, and later Seve Ballesteros, must have gladdened the hearts of those former champions.

Ballesteros came to the 18th on nine over par for the championship. The gallery, knowing they would not be watching him over the week-end, rose. Seve responded by blowing kisses to all sides. "The reaction of the spectators was the only good thing about the week," Ballesteros said. "But their support was not enough for me to play better. I still love this place and the people were wonderful."

Earlier, there had been no need for sentiment. Nostalgia, maybe, but the reaction Nicklaus received was to acclaim an inspired round of golf, a five-under-par 66. At seven under for the championship, he was just one stroke behind the young Irishman, Paul McGinley, at the top of the leaderboard. For some, was it not always like this? For others, it was a reminder of their youth. For the Ballesteros generation, it was a chance to cherish a memory that has not been gleaned from history book or archive video.

Now 56 years of age, Nicklaus was having fun again. "That's why I'm here," he said. "Aren't you supposed to have fun? Don't you enjoy 66s? If that's a form of torture, then torture me every day. No, that's why you come — you want to have fun. The people were wonderful, terrific. But it's no fun waving to them when you're finishing at noon on Sunday, or finishing at noon on Friday before you set off

home. But when you are playing well and you're in contention, hell, that's what you come for. That's what I've played 40 years for. It's been awhile since I've had such fun."

But with Nicklaus, just being here to wave to the crowd is not enough. "I think the ovation was fantastic, but that's an expensive ovation! If you were to put the gas in my aeroplane, pay my hotel bill, pay for all my kids and so on. Seriously, though, I enjoy coming if I can compete, that's always been my criteria. I've never been one to become a ceremonial golfer. I have said all along that I would have a very hard time with that. I thought I was getting awfully close, maybe I am there, but for a ceremonial golfer, I'm doing pretty good this week."

As Arnold Palmer made a very ceremonial, and emotional, farewell to the Open at St Andrews, Nicklaus voiced doubts about whether he would return to the Open on a regular basis. Only at the US Open in June, when he slogged round the monster of Oakland Hills as well as players halfway his age, did he confirm he would be coming to Lytham. Even on his two previous outings, in the US Senior Open and the Ford Senior Players Championship, there were doubts as to whether he thought he was playing well enough. "I had 23 seniors beat me last week, and 15 the week before. Yeah, that gave me a lot of confidence." But he did come. The only explanation is that the day he thinks he is not competitive is the day Jack Nicklaus tees up with Harry Vardon and Walter Hagen in a celestial threeball. And even then …

This was to be Nicklaus' 35th consecutive Open Championship. The previous 34 had brought three victories, at Muirfield in 1966, and at St Andrews in 1970 and 1978. He had been second seven times, including at Lytham in 1963, the only time he bogeyed the last two holes to lose a major, and in 1979. There were also three third places, including the 1974 Lytham Open. For 15 straight years from 1966,

Nicklaus said he would not come to the Open just for the ovations, "but for a ceremonial golfer, I'm doing pretty good."

he was never out of the top six. In all, he finished in the top-25 21 times and missed the cut only four times, three of them in the 1990s. Who wouldn't want to come back with a record like that?

The first appointments were to watch his son Gary (unsuccessfully) in the final qualifying at St Annes Old Links and then to visit Carden Park, in Cheshire, where he was building a second 18 holes along with another son, Steve. Once he got to Royal Lytham, he liked what he saw, and loved the weather forecast. The sunshine was set for the week and the course was playing hard and fast. "I watched Wimbledon and I knew if it was that bad at Wimbledon, it had to be good this week," Nicklaus said.

"My problem with the British Open is the weather. When it gets cold, I get stiff and I have a horrible time. But I love the forecast and the conditions we're playing right now are similar to those we play on the Senior Tour. The golf course is not overly long and the greens are not overly fast. The difference is that, obviously, you are playing in bunkers and the rough that we don't have. The bunkers dictate exactly what you play off the tee. That is British golf. If I wanted to play a wet golf course I would go play in the States. We come over for seaside golf, dust coming off and the ball bouncing. That is what I enjoy."

But Nicklaus had a problem. His back went during his final practice round in the company of Bob Charles, the 1963 Lytham champion. That night, Nicklaus spoke on the phone to his anatomical functionalist, or physiotherapist, in San Diego on the phone. Peter Egoscue was a major in the Marine Corps in Vietnam before he was shot in both legs. Explained Nicklaus: "They put him back together and he still hurt real bad. He asked why do I still hurt and they said we don't know. He started exercising different muscles and taught himself. Lots of athletes go to him. He has taken me through all the 280 muscles in my back."

Egoscue talked Nicklaus out of spasm on Wednesday evening, but a late tee-time on Thursday proved a godsend. "When I got up this morning, I could not stand up or sit down," Nicklaus said. At 10.30 am, or 2.30 am on the American west coast, he called Egoscue and they talked for an hour. "He took me through a programme of exercises and by the time I got to the first tee I was 80 per cent, and by the time I finished I was 95 per cent. The spasm was in the lower, thoracic back. I have not had this for years. It started about three weeks ago. I think it is fatigue.

"When I got to the course, I felt I didn't want to go out and play two holes and then withdraw and take a spot away from somebody. I was determined that I was either going to play and finish the round or not play at all. I didn't want to play five holes just to say I'd played in 35 consecutive Opens. I've seen guys do that and take a spot away from a younger player."

Nicklaus opened with a two-under-par 69, which could have been better but for a couple of wayward drives on the 15th and 16th. That night he found a 20-page fax from Egoscue when he got home. "I guess he didn't want me phoning him at 2.30 am again," said Nicklaus. He was off at 8.39 the following morning, with the chance to open with two sub-par rounds for the first time since 1970. More pertinently, he had recently noticed a newspaper article which highlighted his tendency to shoot a higher score in the second round than in the first in major championships.

He went to the turn in 32 and returned in 34. He did not drop a shot and it could have been even better. Three putts lipped out on the back nine, including one at the last that would have equalled his best score in the Open. He had shot a final-round 65 in finishing fourth at Royal Troon in 1973, and in the third round at Turnberry in that dramatic duel with Tom Watson in 1977. It was his fifth round of 66. Remarkably, three of them helped him to runner-up finishes. The last time, it was after shooting an 83 in the first round at Sandwich in 1981. Even more astonishingly, his halfway total of 135 was his lowest ever in 35 Opens.

But for Tom Lehman joining McGinley at the top of the leaderboard, Nicklaus would have been in the last group of a major championship on the week-end for possibly the last time in his career. If it was fun on the course, Nicklaus was also having fun in his press conference. When was the last time he felt under pressure? "Last week, when I was playing terrible. Am I feeling any pressure this week? No. I don't feel pressure when I play well, only when I play poorly." When was the last time he felt he could win a British Open after 36 holes? "You'd have to go back a couple of decades. I don't know. I have no idea."

How surprised was he to be in this position? "I'm never surprised if I play well. I'm disappointed if I play poorly. I mean, I've played well before. I know what playing golf feels like and I know what my golf game is like when I play well. I know what I am

Son Steve carried Nicklaus' bag.

inside. I know how I mentally handle it and I know how my composure is. I'm pretty good right now with those elements, even though I'm not hitting the ball well really. Actually, I'm playing terribly, but I managed my game well and I felt like I am getting closer. Now, whether that will continue, who knows what will happen over the next couple of days? If I'm to stay in contention then I have to drive the ball better than I did today. It could be 150 over the next couple of days, I don't know what I'll do."

As it turned out, Nicklaus shot exactly 150 (77, 73) over the week-end. At the first hole on Saturday, he almost holed his bunker shot, then lipped out with the par putt. The next 35 holes followed a similar theme. He finished at one over par, in joint 45th place. "It was fun for the first half of the tournament, but then faded into oblivion," he said. "I got into a very good position and really thought I could do well. I hit the ball decently, but just didn't putt well enough. There is a fine line between putting great and putting mediocre.

"My time is past when it comes to winning majors. Now it is fun as long as I can compete. I'm a bit disappointed. When you finish down in the pack, it is not much fun. I will only come over for the Open if I can compete, but that is the only way I will come." Jack Nicklaus not think he is competitive? It is unthinkable ...

Tom Lehman (198) shot a course-record 64 and said: "I would rather be six strokes ahead than six strokes behind."

# ARE SIX STROKES ENOUGH?

## BY ROBERT SOMMERS

Galleries can be fickle. Today's hero could turn into tomorrow's villain, but in golf at least, it's more often the other way round. It is strange indeed how one player can be unpopular at the beginning of his career and then, as he develops into one of the game's great players, transform into a hero. These conversions happen periodically; perhaps Jack Nicklaus is the best example. Resented when he displaced Arnold Palmer as the absolute ruler of the game, he gradually developed into a revered figure, followed by large groups of fans no matter how well or how badly he's playing.

Nick Faldo is going through the same rebirth. Better liked than when he won his three Open Championships, Faldo drew the largest and most passionate following at Royal Lytham and St Annes. His loyal fans trooped along behind him, raising a choking cloud of dust as they trod the pathway alongside the 11th, cheered his every shot, moaned as the putts slipped past the cup, and generally urged him on, obviously hoping he could win once more and, perhaps, fight off the growing American challenge to the Open Championship. That challenge had grown severe; after 36 holes, six of the 12 leaders were American.

Faldo admitted he had been moved, saying: "They have given me a wonderful reception. They were egging me on all the way round, and in trying to do something for them, I was getting aggressively frustrated. I'm enjoying it very much. The fans have created a great atmosphere. When there are 20,000 people cheering for you it's impossible to keep totally calm, but that's all right. I'm very grateful to everybody."

Faldo's followers have so much faith in him that at the end of the day, after he had shot his third consecutive 68, they seemed immensely pleased, even though he was in second place, and lay six strokes behind Tom Lehman. Remembering how Faldo had

made up six strokes on Greg Norman in the US Masters, they took the attitude that Faldo had Lehman just where he wanted him.

Perhaps they felt that way, but as Lehman said late Saturday afternoon, "I would rather be six strokes ahead than six strokes behind."

Lehman had climbed into the lead with a blistering 64, not only the lowest score of the championship, but the course record as well. His 54-hole score of 198 set the championship record, beating Faldo's 199, which he had set at St Andrews in 1990 and matched at Muirfield two years later. Faldo trailed with 204, with Mark Brooks and Vijay Singh just one stroke behind, at 205, followed by Fred Couples and Ernie Els, at 206.

This had been a grim day for Nicklaus, who had begun the round with so much hope, just one stroke behind the leaders. His driver, which had been unreliable through the first two rounds, turned for the worse. Constantly fighting out of trouble, Nicklaus shot 77 and fell to a joint 34th place, 14 strokes behind Lehman, at 212.

Others had shaky rounds as well. Nobody had expected much of Paul McGinley, who had shared the 36-hole lead, because of his history of weak finishes. He had double-bogeyed the first play-off hole and lost the 1993 French Open to Costantino Rocca, had the 1994 Mediterranean Open won but double-bogeyed the 17th and bogeyed the 18th and lost to Jose Maria Olazabal, then lost a tournament in Perth, Australia, by driving into a bunker on the last hole. Now he started with a peculiar bogey, missing the green, then chipping into a bunker. He had to one-putt to save the 4. At the end of the day he had shot 74 and dropped into a tie for 11th place.

Paul Broadhurst shot 40 on the second nine, and with 74 fell further back. Peter Hedblom raced to the turn in 32 and stood 10 under par, but with a 7 on the 15th and a 6 on the 18th, he came back in 43,

Nick Faldo (204) shot 68 to be in the last group. "If anything is going to happen," he said, "that is the best place to be."

shot 75, and slid to 210 and a tie for 22nd place. Carl Mason had fought to nine under par through the 15th, but the 17th destroyed him once again. He hacked his way to a 7; in three rounds he had needed 19 strokes to play this trying hole. With 70 he finished with 208.

At the same time, others shot disappointing rounds that did them little damage. Out in 34, Mark McCumber didn't birdie a hole on the home nine, shot 37, and with 71 slipped to a tie for seventh place. Ernie Els shot 71 as well but held on to a share of fifth with Fred Couples, who shot 69.

Greg Norman shot 71 too. Usually one of the most visible players, Norman had been relatively obscure through the first two rounds, even though, at 139, he wasn't too far behind. He began the third round as if he were off on another of those blistering rounds he often plays. With four birdies and a single bogey on the fifth, not an easy par 3, Greg turned for home in 32, and right then stood six under par. A few more birdies on the home nine and he would turn into a serious threat, and several holes offered the opportunity. He birdied none of them and in fact bogeyed the 16th, one of those par 4s within reach of a short pitch, came back in 39, and with 71 turned what might have been a sparkling round into another disappointing day.

Usually a deadly putter, Corey Pavin missed one from two feet, and with 74 lost ground he would never make up. Mark O'Meara and Loren Roberts shot 72 and fell back, and Padraig Harrington's 73 ended what had been a promising start.

This day belonged to Tom Lehman; he seized it from the opening shot.

Off last, paired with McGinley, Lehman ripped through the first nine in 30, which truly could not have been better. He had to scramble for his pars on both the fifth and eighth and for his birdie on the sixth, where he bunkered his second shot but dropped a 15-foot putt.

This was Lehman's fourth birdie of the round. He had begun by playing a seven iron onto the first green and then holing from 18 feet for his first birdie. Now, with McGinley's bogey, Lehman had the lead to himself at nine under par.

Mark Brooks (205) struggled for pars on the first nine.

After his 69, Vijay Singh (205) said: "I seem to just have a few loose shots now and then which are costing me dearly."

His drive down the left side of the second stopped only a yard or two short of a fairway bunker, but a nice pitch settled 15 feet from the cup and he birdied again. Ten under par now.

He made a routine 4 at the third, and then from the middle of the fourth fairway Lehman nearly holed his eight-iron second; his pitch rolled within a foot and a half, and Lehman had his third birdie of the day. Now he stood at 11 under par, two strokes ahead of Peter Hedblom, who was still playing well, and three ahead of Faldo, who had played through seven.

Now Lehman made a mistake. His six-iron tee shot to the fifth drifted left and into a bunker, but he recovered nicely and saved his par 3. He was still three under for the round, 11 under for 41 holes. He fought for his birdie 4 at the sixth, holing from 15 feet after his eight-iron second missed the green, and he could do no better than par the seventh, when his second, played from deep grass in the left rough, pulled up just short of a bunker carved into the side of a mound on the right. With the hole set on the left of the green directly behind another bunker cut into a high mound, it was impossible to reach with a pitch. Lehman's shot landed close, but it had nothing on it, ran to the back of the green, and he two-putted for the 5.

Once again he struggled to save a par on the eighth, where, from a decent lie in centre fairway, he pitched short of the green, left an indifferent chip 10 feet short, then ran the putt home. Still four under, he finished the first nine with a perfectly gauged nine-iron shot that braked hole-high about 10 feet left of the cup. Everyone assumed he would make it, and he did — he hadn't missed a holeable putt yet — and slipped to five under for the round, 13 under for 45 holes, and three strokes ahead of Faldo and Hedblom.

While Lehman had holed everything he looked at, Faldo was playing marvellous shots, but he couldn't make a putt. After three opening pars where he had legitimate birdie openings, he lost a stroke at the fourth by three-putting from 18 feet. With the bogey he had fallen back to five under par, but he thrust himself back into the race by flying a nine-iron second to the sixth and running in a 25-foot putt for an

Ernie Els (206) bogeyed three of the first four holes.

With 66, Steve Stricker (207) moved to joint seventh place.

Shigeki Maruyama (207) holed this putt for par on the fifth, shot 69 and tied for seventh.

Darren Clarke (207) holed this birdie at the seventh.

eagle 3, then following with a two-putt birdie at the seventh. When the putt fell, the gallery whooped and cheered and raced ahead to the eighth; their man was in the hunt and they wanted to be there for the kill.

Faldo had a bit of a break on the seventh, but how much it helped is difficult to say. It probably wasn't much. After a good drive he played a four iron that hit short, darted across the green and shot up a rather steep hill rising at the back. As it scooted up the incline, spectators scrambled out of the way, but one fan's foot slipped on the slick grass and appeared to kick the ball. It rolled back down the hill and onto the green. It seemed likely, though, that the ball would have tumbled back onto the green without any help because minutes later Nicklaus overshot the green, and his ball, which didn't climb as high as Faldo's, rolled back as well.

Nevertheless, Faldo made his birdie, then holed a 15-foot putt from the back of the eighth for another. Now he had picked up four strokes in three holes. When he made his par 3 at the ninth, he had gone out in 32 and lost only two strokes to Lehman. But Lehman would continue his assault while Faldo would back off.

After a routine par 4 on the 10th, Lehman laid up with his second shot to the 11th, then pitched to

Fred Couples (206) said: "I didn't get the birdies I needed."

A level-par 71 left Mark McCumber (207) tied for seventh.

Rocco Mediate (208) advanced to joint 11th place with his steady performance.

David Duval (209) had recovered from an opening 76.

Hidemichi Tanaka (208) posted another below-par score.

eight feet. Once again the putt fell, and Tom slipped to 14 under par. He hadn't missed a makeable putt yet. On to the 12th, a devilish par 3 where the flag was set in a dangerous position at the front of the green. Not taking the dare, Lehman played his four iron to the middle of the green and parred, followed with a pitch that rolled to the back of the 13th green, and then missed from about 12 feet, the first makeable putt he had missed.

No matter, he picked up another birdie with a six iron to six feet on the 14th, and added another unlikely birdie at the 16th. All his birdies had been made from holeable distances or close to it; the 18-footer at the first had been the longest. Now he rolled one in from 35 feet, startling even himself. When the putt fell, he dropped his putter, and wearing an expression of genuine amazement, raised his hands and looked heavenward in thanks. He was 16 under par now, eight under for the day. If he could only par the remaining two holes he would shoot 63 and put up a score of 197 for 54 holes.

As Lehman played the 16th, Faldo was finishing the 18th, frustrated by losing ground on the homeward holes. He had played the second nine in 36, level par, but he had given away strokes on both the 14th and 16th, two holes he should have parred. He even had struggled to birdie the 11th after a one-iron second jumped into a greenside bunker. He saved the 4 by holing from 15 feet.

Faldo stood four under par for the day then, four strokes behind Lehman, but he would move no closer. He lost one stroke when he bunkered his approach to the 14th and another on the 16th, one of the few birdie holes on the second nine. When his ball squirted into the bunker on the 14th, Nick hung his head, leaned on his club, and put his right hand on his hip, a perfect picture of disgust.

His bogey on the 16th was hard won. From the right rough, he hit a terrible shot that streaked wildly off-line, shot across the fairway, and dived into one of those steep-faced pot bunkers alongside the green's left side. As the ball plopped into the sand, Faldo, his eyes widening, cried, "I don't believe it." It was true, though, and when he looked he found his ball lying so close to the rear wall he would have to crouch low

Brad Faxon (208) shot 68, level on the second nine.

Mark O'Meara (208) bogeyed the last for 72.

Loren Roberts (208) shot 72 in the third round.

Carl Mason (208) holed this birdie putt at the seventh.

Paul McGinley (208) tumbled to 74 on the third day.

Jack Nicklaus (212) said he had nothing but bad luck.

outside the bunker with his feet splayed and try to chop it out. His first shot didn't make it; the ball ran a few feet along the grass on top and then tumbled back in. His second attempt, his fourth shot, left him a nervous five-footer, but he holed it.

Then, as great players do, Faldo struck back. Playing the 17th perfectly — a one iron from the tee, and then a seven iron that carried to the downslope of a rise on the left and trickled within two feet of the cup. The putt fell, and Faldo was back to three under for the day, nine under for the 53 holes. He might have made it to 10 under, but after two precise shots on the home hole, he left his putt dead in the hole but short. He had shot another 68 and 204 for 54 holes.

Meanwhile, two holes farther back, Lehman laid an eight iron within 15 feet on the treacherous 17th and putted directly at the hole. As the ball glided past the cup, grazing the edge, the gallery gasped; they couldn't believe it didn't fall. Still, he had played 17 holes in eight under par and needed only a 4 on the 18th to shoot 63.

He didn't make it. He tried to fade a drive around a fairway bunker about 240 yards out. The shot

didn't work; it dived into the bunker and Tom had no hope of reaching the green. He pitched out all right, but bogeyed. Instead of 63, he shot 64, still setting the course record and lowering the 54-hole championship record by a stroke.

It had been a wonderful round to watch, filled with sparkling shotmaking and extraordinary putting. Lehman didn't miss one putt he should have made, only two he might have made, and he holed at least one he had no right to expect to make. He admitted as much, saying: "I don't think I could have putted any better. Every putt I hit was in the hole or it felt like it was going in the hole."

Lehman's six-stroke lead was the largest since 1964, when Tony Lema played the first 54 holes in 209 at St Andrews and led Nicklaus by seven strokes. But considering the events of April in Augusta, when Faldo beat Norman by 11 strokes, someone wondered if Tom's six strokes would be enough.

"You mean like lightening striking twice?" Lehman asked. Then he smiled and said: "This is a different time and a different place. I feel like I'm playing very well, and I like my chances."

With the course-record 64 almost in hand, Tom Lehman waved to the cheering crowd as he approached the 18th green.

# THIRD ROUND RESULTS

| HOLE | 1 | 2 | 3 | 4 | 5 | 6 | 7 | 8 | 9 | 10 | 11 | 12 | 13 | 14 | 15 | 16 | 17 | 18 | |
|---|---|---|---|---|---|---|---|---|---|---|---|---|---|---|---|---|---|---|---|
| PAR | 3 | 4 | 4 | 4 | 3 | 5 | 5 | 4 | 3 | 4 | 5 | 3 | 4 | 4 | 4 | 4 | 4 | 4 | TOTAL |
| Tom Lehman | 2 | 3 | 4 | 3 | 3 | 4 | 5 | 4 | 2 | 4 | 4 | 3 | 4 | 3 | 4 | 3 | 4 | 5 | 64-198 |
| Nick Faldo | 3 | 4 | 4 | 5 | 3 | 3 | 4 | 3 | 3 | 4 | 4 | 3 | 4 | 5 | 4 | 5 | 3 | 4 | 68-204 |
| Mark Brooks | 3 | 4 | 4 | 4 | 3 | 4 | 5 | 4 | 3 | 4 | 4 | 3 | 3 | 4 | 4 | 4 | 4 | 4 | 68-205 |
| Vijay Singh | 3 | 5 | 3 | 4 | 2 | 4 | 5 | 5 | 3 | 4 | 4 | 4 | 4 | 5 | 4 | 4 | 3 | 3 | 69-205 |
| Fred Couples | 3 | 4 | 4 | 4 | 3 | 4 | 5 | 3 | 2 | 4 | 5 | 3 | 5 | 4 | 4 | 4 | 4 | 4 | 69-206 |
| Ernie Els | 4 | 4 | 5 | 5 | 3 | 4 | 4 | 4 | 2 | 4 | 5 | 2 | 4 | 5 | 4 | 3 | 5 | 4 | 71-206 |
| Steve Stricker | 2 | 4 | 4 | 4 | 3 | 4 | 4 | 3 | 3 | 4 | 5 | 3 | 4 | 4 | 4 | 4 | 4 | 3 | 66-207 |
| Darren Clarke | 2 | 5 | 4 | 4 | 3 | 5 | 3 | 4 | 3 | 4 | 4 | 3 | 4 | 4 | 4 | 4 | 4 | 5 | 69-207 |
| Shigeki Maruyama | 3 | 4 | 5 | 3 | 3 | 4 | 4 | 5 | 3 | 3 | 4 | 3 | 4 | 4 | 4 | 4 | 4 | 5 | 69-207 |
| Mark McCumber | 3 | 3 | 4 | 4 | 4 | 4 | 6 | 4 | 2 | 4 | 5 | 3 | 4 | 5 | 4 | 4 | 4 | 4 | 71-207 |
| Brad Faxon | 3 | 4 | 4 | 3 | 4 | 4 | 4 | 4 | 2 | 4 | 5 | 3 | 3 | 5 | 4 | 4 | 4 | 4 | 68-208 |
| Rocco Mediate | 3 | 4 | 3 | 6 | 2 | 4 | 5 | 5 | 3 | 4 | 4 | 3 | 4 | 4 | 4 | 4 | 3 | 4 | 69-208 |
| Hidemichi Tanaka | 4 | 4 | 4 | 5 | 3 | 4 | 4 | 5 | 2 | 4 | 3 | 2 | 4 | 4 | 4 | 4 | 5 | 5 | 70-208 |
| Carl Mason | 4 | 3 | 4 | 4 | 2 | 5 | 4 | 3 | 3 | 3 | 5 | 3 | 4 | 4 | 3 | 5 | 7 | 4 | 70-208 |
| Loren Roberts | 3 | 5 | 4 | 4 | 4 | 4 | 5 | 5 | 3 | 4 | 5 | 3 | 3 | 3 | 4 | 4 | 5 | 4 | 72-208 |
| Mark O'Meara | 2 | 4 | 4 | 4 | 4 | 5 | 5 | 4 | 3 | 4 | 4 | 5 | 4 | 4 | 3 | 4 | 4 | 5 | 72-208 |
| Paul McGinley | 4 | 4 | 4 | 3 | 5 | 5 | 4 | 4 | 4 | 3 | 5 | 4 | 4 | 5 | 4 | 4 | 4 | 4 | 74-208 |

# HOLE SUMMARY

| HOLE | PAR | EAGLES | BIRDIES | PARS | BOGEYS | HIGHER | RANK | AVERAGE |
|---|---|---|---|---|---|---|---|---|
| 1 | 3 | 0 | 17 | 45 | 14 | 1 | 12 | 2.99 |
| 2 | 4 | 0 | 15 | 49 | 13 | 0 | 13 | 3.97 |
| 3 | 4 | 0 | 7 | 48 | 20 | 2 | 5 | 4.22 |
| 4 | 4 | 0 | 12 | 49 | 14 | 2 | 8 | 4.08 |
| 5 | 3 | 0 | 12 | 54 | 10 | 1 | 11 | 3.00 |
| 6 | 5 | 4 | 47 | 24 | 2 | 0 | 18 | 4.31 |
| 7 | 5 | 2 | 29 | 37 | 7 | 2 | 17 | 4.73 |
| 8 | 4 | 0 | 11 | 42 | 23 | 1 | 6 | 4.18 |
| 9 | 3 | 0 | 13 | 57 | 5 | 2 | 15 | 2.95 |
| OUT | 35 | 6 | 163 | 405 | 108 | 11 | | 34.43 |
| 10 | 4 | 0 | 8 | 58 | 10 | 1 | 10 | 4.05 |
| 11 | 5 | 1 | 18 | 47 | 10 | 1 | 16 | 4.90 |
| 12 | 3 | 0 | 5 | 51 | 18 | 3 | 1 | 3.25 |
| 13 | 4 | 0 | 16 | 51 | 9 | 1 | 14 | 3.94 |
| 14 | 4 | 0 | 6 | 48 | 22 | 1 | 4 | 4.25 |
| 15 | 4 | 0 | 5 | 59 | 11 | 2 | 7 | 4.14 |
| 16 | 4 | 0 | 11 | 53 | 10 | 3 | 9 | 4.06 |
| 17 | 4 | 0 | 6 | 49 | 17 | 5 | 2 | 4.30 |
| 18 | 4 | 0 | 8 | 44 | 22 | 3 | 3 | 4.26 |
| IN | 36 | 1 | 83 | 460 | 129 | 20 | | 37.15 |
| TOTAL | 71 | 7 | 246 | 865 | 237 | 31 | | 71.58 |

| | | | | |
|---|---|---|---|---|
| Players Below Par | 24 | | | |
| Players At Par | 17 | | | |
| Players Above Par | 36 | | | |

### LOW SCORES

| | | |
|---|---|---|
| Low First Nine | Tom Lehman | 30 |
| Low Second Nine | David Duval | 32 |
| Low Round | Tom Lehman | 64 |

### WEATHER

Dry and sunny again.
Southwesterly breeze becoming
northwesterly in the afternoon.

There were refreshments to suit any taste at the Open Championship.

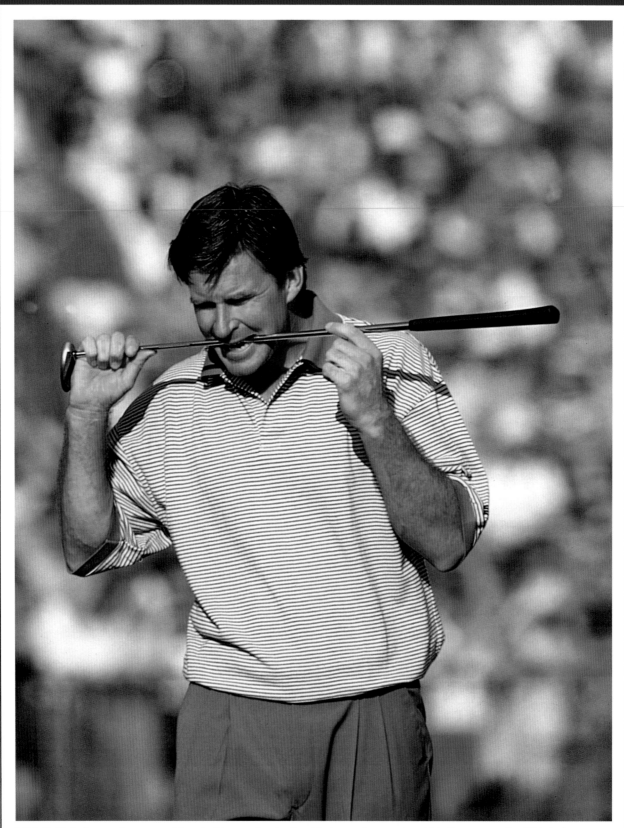

Nick Faldo's frustration was evident in his reaction in the third round to a missed birdie putt on the 18th hole.

# EUROPE ON THE SHORT END

## BY ALISTER NICOL

When Tom Lehman finished runner-up to Jose Maria Olazabal in the 1994 US Masters at Augusta, little serious heed was paid to the man from Minnesota. When Lehman's visit to a bunker on the 72nd hole in this year's US Open at Oakland Hills opened a door through which Steve Jones gratefully strode, there were those who shook their heads and sighed that here was another unfortunate who might be destined to be "always the bridesmaid."

And when that most feared and hardened of competitors, Nick Faldo, finished his third round in the heat of Royal Lytham and St Annes with a birdie-par flourish for his third successive 68, debate in clubhouses, bars and homes was fuelled. After all, only a few months previously hadn't England's greatest-ever golfer overcome a six-shot deficit to trounce Greg Norman at Augusta for his third green jacket? And while Faldo was again six adrift with a round to play, surely Norman must have been a much more formidable figure than Lehman who, while Norman and Faldo were winning major championships, was still fumbling his way round golf's minor circuits.

All of England, and golf for that matter, licked their lips in anticipation. Could Faldo repeat the near-miracle of Augusta? Would Lehman fret and fidget throughout a sleepless night thinking of the dropped shot at his 54th hole which cost him a share of the championship record of 63? Would the burden of that six-stroke advantage prove too heavy for those broad shoulders which twice before had muscled their way within sight of success at the highest level only to sag in defeat? Or would the curse of Lytham be exorcised by Lehman becoming the first American professional to win golf's oldest championship on the bunker-strewn Lancashire links?

Such greats as Arnold Palmer, Jack Nicklaus, Lee Trevino, Tom Watson had all been repelled by Royal Lytham and St Annes in the past, but a close study of the leaderboard that Saturday evening was ominous reading for those non-Americans hoping the Stars and Stripes would once again be lowered. Of the top 10 players only Japan's sturdy Shigeki Maruyama, playing in his first Open, and Darren Clarke of Ulster were not full-time on the US Tour. Of the others hoping to play catch-up on Lehman's lead only Faldo, South African Ernie Els and Fijian Vijay Singh were non-Americans.

Despite Europe's thrilling and well-deserved triumph in last September's Ryder Cup at Oak Hill, the European presence in the shake-up for the 125th Open Championship title was notable only by its absence. Severiano Ballesteros, winner of the two most recent Opens at Lytham and beaten by Lehman in the last-day singles at Oak Hill, failed to recapture any of his 1979 or 1988 magic moments as he strolled, more in desperate hope than anticipation, down Lytham's memory lane. The Spaniard, Europe's captain for next year's Ryder Cup at Valderrama, was a man in anguish. So too was his long-time rival Bernhard Langer. The tough-minded German's ongoing battle against the putting yips were compounded at this year's Open by a suspect back. Seve missed the cut, and Langer withdrew.

Europe's current leaders, Ian Woosnam and Colin Montgomerie, also suffered the ignominy of failing to survive beyond the first two rounds, in stark contrast to Belgium's little-known golfing nomad Arnaud Langenaeken and Scottish club pro Gordon Law, who both came through the pre-qualifying and final qualifying to ensure a working week-end while Woosie flew off back to Jersey and Monty suffered his private torture.

That both are class acts is undeniable. The previous Saturday Woosnam had come through four days of buffeting over the sternest challenge even Carnoustie could present to lift the Scottish Open title for an unprecedented third time and professed

Both of Europe's current leaders, Colin Montgomerie (left) and Ian Woosnam (right) failed to qualify for the final 36 holes.

himself ready for Lytham. He did add the prophetic rider, however, that he had never been a great lover of what he called "sea links golf."

Montgomerie, on the other hand, was ill-prepared to improve on what he referred to as "the worst record of any of the world's top players in the Open." He had failed to get beyond the first two days in three of the last four Open Championships, and following a disastrous 81 on the last day at Carnoustie claimed that the wind had destroyed his swing and that perhaps the course had been overly difficult. By the time he arrived at Lytham it seemed the big Scot was still sadly out of sorts with his game.

The absence of four of Europe's superstars who have eight major championships between them left Faldo a man alone to stem the inexorable American tide. What back-up he had could scarcely be termed formidable. Darren Clarke is a hugely talented and likeable young man with a deep well of potential. Joint overnight leader Dubliner Paul McGinley is still emerging from the journeyman category, while the only other home player high up on the leaderboard on Saturday night, Carl Mason, was just happy to be playing golf at all. At 208 he was 10 strokes

behind leader Lehman, and any dreams the 43-year-old may have entertained about improving on his fourth-place finish behind Tom Watson at Muirfield in 1980 had been cruelly dashed by Lytham's dogleg 17th hole.

Mason had taken a 7 there in Friday's second round of 70, and the nightmare repeated itself on Saturday when, despite a second triple bogey, he again shot 70. Mason is one of the most likeable men in golf with a temperament seemingly as calm as a millpond. He was understandably upset when he came off the course on Saturday evening, but was soon able to accept his twin disasters with philosophical stoicism.

One day Mason stepped out of his car to fill up the fuel tank and by the time he reached the cashier's desk he was doubled up in agony like a half-shut knife. He had damaged a disc. For three tormented weeks he was unable to walk more than 10 yards and feared for his future as a golfer. In total he was out of action for nine weeks and only a slow-release epidural injection enabled Carl to start swinging again. Not surprisingly he went into the Open with no great burden of expectation.

His 7 at the 17th on Saturday could not have been more different to Faldo's impeccable birdie 3. Mason's one-iron tee shot found one of the dreaded bunkers. He needed four more shots to reach the putting surface, including a duffed chip, and two putts later it all added up to a 7. Faldo, on the other hand, struck a magnificent long-iron second shot to within two feet of the cup for a "gimme" birdie and gained four shots on his countryman at one hole.

Looking more relaxed than has often been the case in the past, Faldo knew before he teed off in the third round that to stay in the hunt for the claret jug he would need to, at the very least, maintain the momentum which had seen him card two 68s in the opening rounds. He dropped a stroke at the fourth hole but picked up four shots in three holes with the aid of an eagle 3 at the long sixth. Meantime Lehman was enjoying one of those days with the putter which even putting wizards such as Ben Crenshaw dream about.

Bernhard Langer withdrew with a back injury.

Faldo fully appreciated the enormity of the task ahead of him in Sunday's last round and brushed aside comparisons with his Masters come-back which eclipsed Norman. "It is a different period of time and a different golf course," he stressed. "I have to go out and shoot a great round and see what happens. Tom will be under enormous pressure. He is going for his first major, while I have it all to gain and nothing to lose. I will need at least a 63."

While conceding that was more of a possibility than a probability, three-time champion Faldo had set his target. Lehman, on the other hand, was mentally cushioned by the improbability of lightning striking twice and by the additional fact that in none of the previous 124 Opens had a player lost a six-stroke advantage.

This Open Championship will long be remembered for the unrelenting heat which was more Lanzarote than Lancashire. In hindsight it might even mark a watershed for European golf, which had been on an unprecedented high since Ballesteros weaved his magic spell over Royal Lytham and St Annes in 1979 and enchanted the entire golfing world. There was little evidence of the mighty European battalions in 1996.

Darren Clarke joined Faldo in the top 10 after 54 holes.

"It really is the greatest day in my life," Tom Lehman said. "It was not pretty but it was gritty. I hung in there as I felt I did not have my game. But it is a dream come true."

# LEHMAN NEED FEAR NO MORE

## BY ROBERT SOMMERS

Fear is a vicious slavemaster, more cruel than any other. Fear of failure is the worst. It can turn some men into quavering, emotional wrecks; and yet it can be the most powerful stimulus of all, driving others to extend themselves, to reach for goals they may never have dreamt of and do things they didn't know they could do.

As an obscure journeyman struggling on the American mini-tours, where the players often competed for their own money, Tom Lehman didn't dream he would ever compete for the world's greatest championship. Once he played himself into position to win, he was afraid he might not. He had come close in important championships in the past and yet he had failed. Only three weeks earlier he had placed second in the US Open, losing a chance to force a play-off by driving into a bunker on the final hole. A year earlier he had played a loose final round in the US Open and placed third, and he had lost the 1994 US Masters by one stroke with a final round of 72 when Jose Maria Olazabal had shot 70.

Now, with one round to play in the Open Championship, and paired with Nick Faldo, who was in second place, six strokes behind, Lehman told himself he didn't want his gravestone to read: "Here Lies Tom Lehman. He Couldn't Win The Big One."

Now there will be no need, for Lehman did indeed win the Open; even though he played his worst golf of the four rounds and shot 73, it was good enough. With a 72-hole score of 271, he scored two strokes better than anyone else.

Others had their chances, but Lehman had carried such a sizeable lead into the final 18 holes only a miracle round would deny him the championship. There were no miracle rounds.

Assessing his position after 54 holes, Faldo had assumed he would have to shoot 63 to catch up. As the round played out he would have needed nothing quite so grand. A 66 would have done the trick, but Faldo shot 70 instead and dropped to fourth place, behind both Mark McCumber and Ernie Els.

Having one of those days when the coordination isn't quite there and the putter feels like a hunk of lead, Lehman was vulnerable if only one of the closest challengers could put pressure on him, but no one within range had the stamina to make him crack. Several made runs at him, but every challenge died. Fred Couples sped round the first nine in 30 and at one stage had climbed within two strokes of Lehman, but he played absolute rubbish on the second nine and fell aside. Mark Brooks closed to 11 under par with three early birdies, but he had nothing in reserve, closed with two disappointing bogeys, and shot 276. Brooks tied Jeff Maggert, another American, whose 65 stood as the best round of the day. Maggert had started too far behind, though, to threaten Lehman.

Els had the best opportunity. Thirteen under par, within two strokes of Lehman with three holes to play, he needed birdies, but instead he bogeyed the 16th and 18th and shot 67, not good enough. Never really on the fringes of the challengers, Greg Norman roused himself as well, shot 67 when it didn't matter, and slipped into a tie for seventh place with Couples, Greg Turner and Peter Hedblom, who also shot 67.

In the end the championship was won by Lehman's firm strength of will, his absolute refusal to give in, and his confidence that he could win an important championship. His golf wasn't the prettiest we had seen throughout the week, but it was effective. He missed only three greens, not including the 14th where his approach rolled just a little over the back. He putted, nevertheless.

Overall his putting could have been better. While he holed only one makeable putt for a birdie, from 15 feet on the 12th, he missed others from 15 feet on the fourth, from seven feet on the eighth, and from 12 feet on the 13th. Still, it was his putter that

Ernie Els (273) was in contention until making bogeys at the 16th and again here at the 18th.

actually saved him. Constantly bold with his first putts, he saved pars on three holes by running in second putts of from four to six feet.

He made the first of these nerve-wracking putts on the first hole.

Off last, behind Brooks and Vijay Singh, Lehman and Faldo were ready to play when they were interrupted by cheering from the 18th, where Jack Nicklaus was playing. As Nicklaus progressed down the last fairway, the cheering grew, and even those seated in the grandstands behind the first hole, or standing alongside the green, turned toward the 18th and applauded as the greatest player of his time played out his round.

When the cheering died, Faldo stepped up and played a precise iron shot within six feet of the cup. Lehman left his ball outside Faldo's, then rammed his approach putt six feet past.

This looked like the kind of opening Faldo needed if he was to cut into Lehman's big lead. He set up to the ball, anchoring himself firmly in place, seemed to stroke the ball nicely, but it eased past the cup. Now Lehman faced a test of nerves on the very first hole.

Standing nearby, tall and lean David Leadbetter, Faldo's coach, muttered, "You don't want these so soon," then added, "but of course they're great if you hole them." Lehman did indeed hole it for the par 3.

Lehman and Faldo were a contrasting pair, Faldo at 6-foot-3, broad-shouldered, regally dressed in well-tailored, colour coordinated clothes, and with a full head of dark brown hair, Lehman an inch shorter, balding, more slope-shouldered and shaggy haired, wearing baggy, off-the-rack khaki trousers, a white shirt intentionally designed to appear too big, and a baseball cap; stylish elegance beside studied casualness.

Their swings mirrored their appearance, Faldo with an elegant, orthodox movement that produced one crisply hit shot after another, Lehman with his own method that projects the image of a heavyweight delivering an upper-cut with a sledge-hammer.

Nevertheless Lehman held the advantage; everyone wondered if he could hold it, for Faldo seemed all business. With the crowd cheering him on, he strode ahead, looking neither right nor left, took

Mark McCumber (273) finished with 66 to tie for second place. Scheduled for shoulder surgery that will keep him out of golf for six months, McCumber said: "If it had been cold weather, I could not have played."

Nick Faldo (274) could not find his putting touch, and shot 70 to finish fourth. "I had so many chances today," Faldo said, "and I was unable to take them. It was as simple as that. It could have been very different."

Mark Brooks (276) had bogeys on the last two holes to tie for fifth place with fellow American Jeff Maggert, who shot a final-round 65.

whatever time he wanted to plan and execute his shots, and generally ignored Lehman, who plodded along and, to his credit, ignored Faldo as well. After Tom had played his approach onto the second, a lone spectator called, "Come on, Tom." Lehman smiled and held up his right index finger, indicting one hole behind him, only 17 more to go.

Still six strokes ahead of Faldo, with the vision of Augusta never far from anyone's mind, Lehman gave the first indication everything wasn't well on the third by pulling his drive into the fairway bunker positioned 250 yards out from the tee. There was no way to reach the green from there. Lehman stood with his right foot in the sand, his left knee against the rising ground, and could do no more than pop the ball out. He bogeyed, Faldo parred, and now Lehman's lead was down to five.

It was cut to four when Faldo played a crisp six iron to 12 feet for a birdie 3 on the fourth, and Faldo seemed assured of picking up another stroke with a stunning iron into the fifth, the 212-yard par 3, that braked about six feet right of the hole. Lehman ran another putt four feet past. Now Faldo. He studied the putt carefully and stroked it perfectly. The ball

ran to the hole, ducked in, then spun out. The crowd moaned and Faldo stared as if he couldn't believe it. He tapped it in, Lehman holed, and they moved on.

The entire complexion of the championship changed on the sixth. It was here that Lehman showed a resoluteness of character that certified he would not cave in; if someone else wanted the championship, they would have to fight him for it. It was here, too, that Faldo showed this would not be his day. Up first, Nick played a daring drive that carried over the knoll on the left with a bunker hollowed into its face, to a perfect position in the fairway. Lehman, though, hooked his drive into what looked at first an unplayable position. The ball dived into a copse of low-growing plane and pine trees and lay under leaves and twigs. Now he faced the question of whether he could play any shot at all.

Luckily, he had an opening, but he couldn't take a full swing. Instead he punched a shot about 30 or 40 yards farther toward the green, but his ball still lay in the rough.

Faldo played next, and from a clean lie hit a seven iron that carried onto the green but rolled off the back and down a slight incline. Lehman's third

Fred Couples (277) went out in 30 to be within two, but came back in 41 including a bogey here on the 11th hole.

Greg Turner (277) shot a second successive 68.

Greg Norman (277) shot 67 after going out in 31.

stopped short, only a yard or so right of a greenside bunker, and he chipped up to six feet. Faldo played a little pitch to three feet, and when Lehman holed for his par 5, once more Faldo looked as if he would cut another stroke from Lehman's lead. Again, though, his ball hit the inside of the cup and flipped out.

Faldo's ball-striking had been as good as ever; he had consistently played irons within birdie range, but on the other hand, his putting had not been what we've come to expect. With all those opportunities he had holed only one putt. At the beginning Leadbetter had said: "The first six to seven holes are crucial. Nick just needs a few early putts." So far he had missed from six feet on the first, from about 10 feet on the second, from six feet on the fifth, and from not much more than three feet on the sixth. Then he missed another birdie opportunity from six feet on the seventh.

Now a look at the scoreboard showed that rather than challenging Lehman, Faldo had dropped to fourth place; while everyone had become engrossed with the ghost of Augusta, Couples had run wild, and Brooks wasn't far behind. With Lehman at 14

under par, Couples had climbed within two strokes of him at 12 under, Brooks was 11 under, and Faldo 10 under par, tied with McCumber. Instead of fighting off one man, Lehman was under siege from four others, with Els about to make his move. Instead of a runaway, the Open had turned into another tense, tight struggle.

Although he is without question among the game's best players, Couples was an unlikely challenger because he had played so little tournament golf over the previous two months. Always susceptible to back stress, he had strained a muscle on the 20th of May and didn't play against until the Motorola Western Open, the week before the Open Championship. In the interval, he had not been fit enough to play in the US Open.

In the first three rounds at Lytham, Fred had shot 67, 70 and 69, and now he was playing marvellous golf. Starting 20 minutes ahead of Lehman and Faldo, Couples opened by holing from 20 feet on the first, from 10 feet on the fourth, made a 2 on the fifth, had nothing but a pitch left to the sixth and birdied again, missed another opportunity on the seventh, and lofted

Mark McNulty (279) had four steady rounds.

Darren Clarke (278) finished with level-par 71.

Vijay Singh (278) shot 73 and dropped from joint third to joint 11th place.

Peter Hedblom (277) improved eight shots to 67.

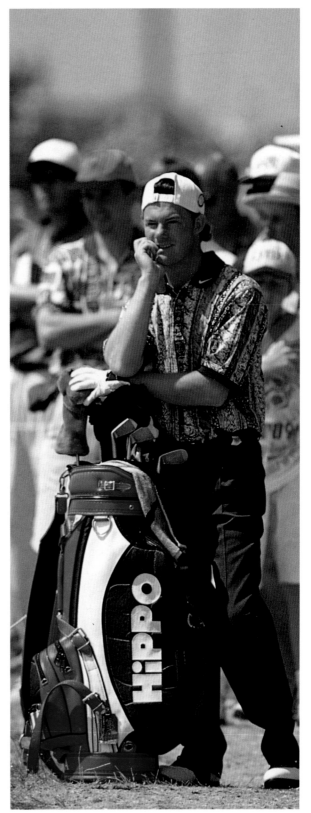

Alexander Cejka (278) shot 67s in two rounds.

a pitch within six or eight feet on the ninth and made his fifth birdie.

Out in 30, he had picked up six strokes on Lehman and climbed from a tie for fifth into second place. But he could go no further. He bogeyed the vulnerable 10th by overshooting the green, then bogeyed the 11th by driving into the dangerous bunker on the left, and then playing a timid little pitch that didn't reach the green from no more than 10 yards. With his ball in a fluffy lie, his club seemed to slip under the ball and missed solid contact. Couples was finished now; with three more bogeys, he came back in 41, and with 277, tied for seventh place.

Brooks too had gone as far as he would go. A slightly built 35-year-old Texan, he prepares for the Open as only a few other Americans. He comes over early and plays a number of links courses to acclimate himself. Not exempt in 1995, he had to pre-qualify, and he very nearly won. He missed the play-off by one stroke after driving into Bishop Sime, a bunker on the 16th at St Andrews. Now he was running up a remarkable record at Lytham. Through 61 holes he stood at 11 under par and hadn't three-putted a hole. He began slipping back when his pitch to the uphill eighth didn't reach level ground and rolled 20 yards back down the hill, costing him a bogey 5, and he couldn't make another birdie. In the end he finished with bogeys on the two closing holes, and with 71 shot 276, tied with Maggert, who had

With two strokes in hand, Lehman could enjoy the rousing ovation that Open champions traditionally receive.

At 6.32, Lehman had secured the Open title.

Tiger Woods received the low amateur medal from Michael Bonallack, secretary of the R and A.

finished earlier. Ties for third and fifth in successive Opens isn't a bad record.

Meantime, Lehman and Faldo struggled on. Faldo finally made a birdie putt, holing from 15 feet on the ninth, but neither man birdied either the 10th or the 11th. Then Lehman played the shot that not only won him an extra stroke but buoyed his spirit as well and gave him a surge of confidence. With half a dozen players closing in, he hit a stunning four iron to the 12th that braked about 12 feet right of the flagstick. When he holed the putt he stood at level par for the day and 15 under for the championship.

It would be enough to see him through. Even a three-putt bogey at the 14th, where he missed from five feet, did little damage. Minutes later Faldo realised his challenge had ended when he drove into a fairway bunker on the 15th. As the ball dived into the sand, Nick's shoulders sagged, and he hung his head.

Meantime Els had made up ground with an outward 33, then birdied four more holes on the second nine, his last on the 15th, where he had lofted an eight iron to four feet. The birdie dropped him to 13 under, still two strokes behind since Lehman hadn't yet bogeyed the 14th, but Els as well would go no further. Right away he drove into a fairway bunker and bogeyed the 16th, then faded another drive into a fairway bunker at the 18th and bogeyed again. At 273 he had tied McCumber. Their only chance now was for Lehman to collapse.

Lehman, though, would not give in. A nice pitch from a bunker saved his par on the 15th; a safe one iron and wedge to the 16th and he had another par, but then he hit a drive into the bunkers at the 17th, where the fairway makes its turn. With three strokes in hand, he accepted the bogey and used one of those strokes to play safely out.

Now he had reached the 18th tee holding a two-stroke lead. With the end in sight he guided a one iron into the rough along the left to avoid the bunkers, and an eight iron to the front of the green, leaving himself in the comfortable position of knowing he could three-putt and still win. He needed only two, shot 73 for the day, two over a lenient par, and won the championship with 271.

As usual that day, Faldo had laid his approach inside Lehman's, but as he walked past he patted Tom on the back and said: "Well done; you deserve to win." This was a common assessment. Certainly the gallery agreed, cheering as Lehman took off his cap, waved to them, and even threw them a few kisses.

When the trophy had been presented, Lehman said: "I can't describe the way I feel. It was a struggle. I didn't play at all well, but I stuck it out, and I came through." Clutching the silver claret jug with his name freshly engraved on the plinth, Lehman went on: "To win this silver trophy and to take it home as Open champion makes all the hard work that led to this day and everything in the past worthwhile."

Finally, he need know fear no more. He had indeed won the big one.

The crowd rose from the stands flanking Royal Lytham's 18th hole to applaud the winner of the 125th Open Championship.

# FOURTH ROUND RESULTS

| HOLE | 1 | 2 | 3 | 4 | 5 | 6 | 7 | 8 | 9 | 10 | 11 | 12 | 13 | 14 | 15 | 16 | 17 | 18 | |
|---|---|---|---|---|---|---|---|---|---|---|---|---|---|---|---|---|---|---|---|
| PAR | 3 | 4 | 4 | 4 | 3 | 5 | 5 | 4 | 3 | 4 | 5 | 3 | 4 | 4 | 4 | 4 | 4 | 4 | TOTAL |
| Tom Lehman | 3 | 4 | 5 | 4 | 3 | 5 | 5 | 4 | 3 | 4 | 5 | 2 | 4 | 5 | 4 | 4 | 5 | 4 | 73-271 |
| Mark McCumber | 3 | 4 | 4 | 4 | 3 | 4 | 4 | 3 | 3 | 4 | 4 | 3 | 4 | 3 | 5 | 3 | 4 | 4 | 66-273 |
| Ernie Els | 3 | 3 | 5 | 4 | 3 | 4 | 4 | 4 | 3 | 3 | 5 | 2 | 3 | 4 | 3 | 5 | 4 | 5 | 67-273 |
| Nick Faldo | 3 | 4 | 4 | 3 | 3 | 5 | 5 | 4 | 2 | 4 | 5 | 3 | 4 | 4 | 5 | 4 | 4 | 4 | 70-274 |
| Jeff Maggert | 2 | 3 | 4 | 4 | 3 | 5 | 4 | 3 | 4 | 4 | 4 | 3 | 2 | 5 | 4 | 3 | 4 | 4 | 65-276 |
| Mark Brooks | 3 | 3 | 4 | 3 | 3 | 4 | 5 | 5 | 3 | 4 | 5 | 3 | 4 | 4 | 4 | 4 | 5 | 5 | 71-276 |
| Peter Hedblom | 3 | 4 | 4 | 4 | 2 | 3 | 5 | 4 | 3 | 4 | 5 | 3 | 3 | 4 | 5 | 3 | 4 | 4 | 67-277 |
| Greg Norman | 4 | 3 | 3 | 4 | 4 | 4 | 3 | 4 | 2 | 4 | 4 | 3 | 4 | 5 | 5 | 4 | 3 | 4 | 67-277 |
| Greg Turner | 3 | 5 | 3 | 4 | 3 | 4 | 5 | 5 | 2 | 4 | 4 | 3 | 3 | 4 | 3 | 4 | 4 | 5 | 68-277 |
| Fred Couples | 2 | 4 | 4 | 3 | 2 | 4 | 5 | 4 | 2 | 5 | 6 | 3 | 5 | 4 | 4 | 4 | 5 | 5 | 71-277 |
| Alexander Cejka | 2 | 4 | 4 | 4 | 3 | 4 | 4 | 4 | 3 | 4 | 5 | 3 | 4 | 5 | 4 | 3 | 3 | 4 | 67-278 |
| Darren Clarke | 3 | 4 | 4 | 4 | 4 | 4 | 5 | 4 | 3 | 5 | 5 | 3 | 3 | 4 | 3 | 4 | 4 | 5 | 71-278 |
| Vijay Singh | 3 | 4 | 4 | 4 | 3 | 6 | 4 | 4 | 3 | 5 | 5 | 3 | 4 | 4 | 4 | 4 | 5 | 4 | 73-278 |

# HOLE SUMMARY

| HOLE | PAR | EAGLES | BIRDIES | PARS | BOGEYS | HIGHER | RANK | AVERAGE |
|---|---|---|---|---|---|---|---|---|
| 1 | 3 | 0 | 6 | 64 | 6 | 1 | 12 | 3.03 |
| 2 | 4 | 0 | 7 | 54 | 14 | 2 | 9 | 4.16 |
| 3 | 4 | 0 | 11 | 45 | 16 | 5 | 5 | 4.22 |
| 4 | 4 | 0 | 10 | 51 | 15 | 1 | 10 | 4.09 |
| 5 | 3 | 0 | 5 | 52 | 20 | 0 | 3 | 3.19 |
| 6 | 5 | 4 | 40 | 26 | 5 | 2 | 17 | 4.49 |
| 7 | 5 | 6 | 34 | 32 | 5 | 0 | 18 | 4.47 |
| 8 | 4 | 0 | 4 | 52 | 19 | 2 | 4 | 4.25 |
| 9 | 3 | 0 | 21 | 50 | 6 | 0 | 16 | 2.81 |
| OUT | 35 | 10 | 138 | 426 | 106 | 13 | | 34.71 |
| 10 | 4 | 0 | 10 | 54 | 12 | 1 | 11 | 4.05 |
| 11 | 5 | 1 | 18 | 45 | 12 | 1 | 13 | 4.92 |
| 12 | 3 | 0 | 7 | 51 | 19 | 0 | 7 | 3.16 |
| 13 | 4 | 1 | 23 | 44 | 9 | 0 | 15 | 3.79 |
| 14 | 4 | 0 | 6 | 51 | 17 | 3 | 5 | 4.22 |
| 15 | 4 | 0 | 9 | 44 | 23 | 1 | 8 | 4.21 |
| 16 | 4 | 0 | 15 | 54 | 7 | 1 | 14 | 3.92 |
| 17 | 4 | 0 | 6 | 47 | 17 | 7 | 1 | 4.34 |
| 18 | 4 | 0 | 2 | 55 | 18 | 2 | 2 | 4.26 |
| IN | 36 | 2 | 96 | 445 | 134 | 16 | | 36.87 |
| TOTAL | 71 | 12 | 234 | 871 | 240 | 29 | | 71.58 |

| | | | | |
|---|---|---|---|---|
| Players Below Par | 28 | | LOW SCORES | |
| Players At Par | 10 | Low First Nine | Fred Couples | 30 |
| Players Above Par | 39 | Low Second Nine | Mark Calcavecchia | 32 |
| | | Low Round | Jeff Maggert | 65 |

## WEATHER

Dry with hazy sunshine.
Wind light and variable.

# CHAMPIONSHIP HOLE SUMMARY

| HOLE | PAR | YARDS | EAGLES | BIRDIES | PARS | BOGEYS | HIGHER | RANK | AVERAGE |
|------|-----|-------|--------|---------|------|--------|--------|------|---------|
| 1 | 3 | 206 | 0 | 57 | 321 | 78 | 9 | 10 | 3.08 |
| 2 | 4 | 437 | 0 | 47 | 320 | 89 | 9 | 8 | 4.13 |
| 3 | 4 | 457 | 0 | 42 | 279 | 122 | 22 | 4 | 4.28 |
| 4 | 4 | 393 | 0 | 70 | 316 | 75 | 4 | 11 | 4.03 |
| 5 | 3 | 212 | 0 | 41 | 310 | 109 | 5 | 6 | 3.17 |
| 6 | 5 | 490 | 24 | 229 | 178 | 30 | 4 | 18 | 4.49 |
| 7 | 5 | 553 | 21 | 196 | 209 | 32 | 7 | 17 | 4.59 |
| 8 | 4 | 418 | 0 | 47 | 288 | 116 | 14 | 7 | 4.21 |
| 9 | 3 | 164 | 1 | 81 | 328 | 50 | 5 | 15 | 2.95 |
| OUT | 35 | 3330 | 46 | 810 | 2549 | 701 | 79 | | 34.93 |
| 10 | 4 | 334 | 0 | 88 | 314 | 59 | 4 | 13 | 3.95 |
| 11 | 5 | 542 | 5 | 151 | 237 | 62 | 10 | 16 | 4.83 |
| 12 | 3 | 198 | 0 | 35 | 298 | 124 | 8 | 2 | 3.23 |
| 13 | 4 | 342 | 2 | 100 | 294 | 59 | 10 | 13 | 3.95 |
| 14 | 4 | 445 | 0 | 48 | 322 | 86 | 9 | 9 | 4.12 |
| 15 | 4 | 463 | 0 | 33 | 289 | 122 | 21 | 3 | 4.29 |
| 16 | 4 | 357 | 1 | 93 | 303 | 60 | 8 | 12 | 3.96 |
| 17 | 4 | 467 | 0 | 41 | 259 | 128 | 37 | 1 | 4.37 |
| 18 | 4 | 414 | 0 | 42 | 290 | 114 | 19 | 5 | 4.24 |
| IN | 36 | 3562 | 8 | 631 | 2606 | 814 | 126 | | 36.94 |
| TOTAL | 71 | 6892 | 54 | 1441 | 5155 | 1515 | 205 | | 71.87 |

| | FIRST ROUND | SECOND ROUND | THIRD ROUND | FOURTH ROUND | TOTAL |
|---|---|---|---|---|---|
| Players Below Par | 42 | 57 | 24 | 28 | 151 |
| Players At Par | 20 | 14 | 17 | 10 | 61 |
| Players Above Par | 94 | 84 | 36 | 39 | 253 |

# RELATIVE DIFFICULTY OF HOLES

| HOLE | PAR | FIRST ROUND | SECOND ROUND | THIRD ROUND | FOURTH ROUND | OVERALL RANK |
|------|-----|-------------|--------------|-------------|--------------|--------------|
| 1 | 3 | 9 | 9 | 12 | 12 | 10 |
| 2 | 4 | 8 | 7 | 13 | 9 | 8 |
| 3 | 4 | 3 | 4 | 5 | 5 | 4 |
| 4 | 4 | 12 | 12 | 8 | 10 | 11 |
| 5 | 3 | 7 | 1 | 11 | 3 | 6 |
| 6 | 5 | 18 | 18 | 18 | 17 | 18 |
| 7 | 5 | 17 | 17 | 17 | 18 | 17 |
| 8 | 4 | 6 | 7 | 6 | 4 | 7 |
| 9 | 3 | 11 | 14 | 15 | 16 | 15 |
| 10 | 4 | 15 | 13 | 10 | 11 | 13 |
| 11 | 5 | 16 | 16 | 16 | 13 | 16 |
| 12 | 3 | 4 | 2 | 1 | 7 | 2 |
| 13 | 4 | 14 | 11 | 14 | 15 | 13 |
| 14 | 4 | 10 | 10 | 4 | 5 | 9 |
| 15 | 4 | 1 | 5 | 7 | 8 | 3 |
| 16 | 4 | 12 | 15 | 9 | 14 | 12 |
| 17 | 4 | 2 | 3 | 2 | 1 | 1 |
| 18 | 4 | 5 | 6 | 3 | 2 | 5 |

The first American professional to win at Royal Lytham, Tom Lehman was a popular champion.

## COMMENTARY

# A YEOMAN CHAMPION

### BY JOHN HOPKINS

We are the children of our parents, bred and brought up by them, taught, educated and influenced by them. From our first steps to their last breaths, we are as much theirs as they are ours. So the pleasure on Jim Lehman's face as he walked round Lytham on Sunday afternoon was understandable.

Jim Lehman looked as his son Tom will in 25 years' time. The only difference was that on this occasion Jim Lehman looked as though he was fit to burst with pride at his son's achievement at becoming the first American professional to win at Royal Lytham and St Annes.

Tom Lehman looks, sounds and dresses like one of America's yeomen, a man on whose broad shoulders the west was won, a man to give a job to and know that it will get done. This is what happened on Sunday. Just after lunch he rolled up his sleeves and started the job in hand and just before dinner he had got it done. At 2.30 he was still the nearly man, the man who was due to win a major championship after going so close so often. At half past 6 o'clock on a lovely afternoon he was the Open champion.

Even in a sport which is notable for the integrity of its competitors, Lehman stands out, and it is easy to see why from the photographs of him in victory. Notice the look of genuine happiness on his face as he cradles the claret jug. Notice that there is an absence of anything suggesting cockiness, an excess of exuberance. The photographs suggest that here is a man who knows how hard he has worked to win this trophy, what he has had to endure before he could put his hands round it and claim it as his own, and this will not distort his future life nor colour his present. The down-to-earth principles that have guided him so far will remain in place in the coming years. Some heads are turned by success but not Tom Lehman's.

On Friday evening after his second successive 67 had put him in a tie with Paul McGinley for the lead on eight under par, Lehman said he thought it was about time an American won the Open. Hang on a minute Tom, someone said. What about John Daly at St Andrews last year? Lehman blushed. He had not mean to slight Daly. He was referring, slightly inaccurately as it happens, to the 70 years of Opens at Lytham without a victory by an American professional. "Oh my," he said. "Don't tell John Daly I said that." It was about the only mistake Lehman made all the time he was in Lancashire.

Could Lehman have won at any other Open venue? Of course he could because he has all the tools the modern champion needs. He is long, strong and straight and, as he demonstrated so convincingly on Saturday afternoon when he took 11 single putts while setting a new course record of 64, he has the facility that big strong men so often have of being able to play with a breathtaking softness and delicacy at times.

But isn't there something apposite in the fact that this yeoman figure won on a course first built by men who toiled in the cotton mills and industrial factories of Manchester and Liverpool and, having made their money doing so, began to think of ways of entertaining themselves at the week-ends when they retired to their bijou residences in the genteel seaside towns of Lytham and St Annes?

"Tom is a fierce competitor," Jack Nicklaus said of Lehman. "He has all the shots and he's tough as we saw in the Ryder Cup. He's not a natural so he's had to pay his dues, and he has had to play his best to win. Like Corey Pavin and Tom Kite and Hale Irwin he has had to work at it. But then so did Ben Hogan."

Hogan lost the US Masters twice by three-putting the final green. Lehman lost the 1994 Masters to Jose Maria Olazabal because, on the day, the Spaniard was able to produce the spark of excellence that ensures that one man becomes champion and an-

Jim Lehman congratulated his son on the victory.

other runner-up, a spark of excellence that Lehman could not match. To win, one usually has to lose first, as Olazabal had at Augusta in 1991 and as Lehman had in 1994, at the 1995 US Open at Shinnecock Hills and the 1996 US Open at Oakland Hills.

But whereas Lehman admitted he had not played well at Shinnecock and was fortunate to be among the leaders, the 1994 Masters and the 1996 US Open were, he felt, opportunities to win that he had let slip. "Losing the Masters hurt because I felt I could have been a little more aggressive," Lehman said. "Oakland Hills hurt me because I felt I had the right attitude and I had courage. That is when it is really painful — when you play close to your best and your best isn't close enough."

This is why it was so important for Lehman that this time he was resolute and skilful enough to hold on to his six-stroke lead over Faldo and to repel any other challengers as well. He remembered what had happened at the US Masters in April when Faldo reeled in Greg Norman's six-stroke lead and turned it into victory by five strokes. Lehman did not need any reminding of the similarities.

He went out and won in a way that was pure Tom Lehman, worthy of the man. It was not spectacular, like Johnny Miller's 63 at Oakmont in 1973 or Seve Ballesteros' 65 at Lytham eight years earlier or Norman's 64 at Royal St George's in 1993. Lehman did it by demonstrating the very virtues on the course that he personifies off it. He was dogged and steady, keeping his head while five men had a run at him. If you can tell a book by its cover, you can tell Tom Lehman by his swing.

"It may not be pretty but it works," Lehman said. "If you have a swing that will repeat and hold up, you start to believe in it. If you hit a couple of good shots and hole a couple of putts, you start to believe in yourself. Then you get close in major championships and then you get to the point where there is no one who can beat you."

On Friday night when he was a joint leader, Lehman said: "I can't pay attention to anyone. If I thought about all the guys who were tied with me or behind me when I was playing well, I probably wouldn't be able to take the club back. I have a lot of respect for a lot of players, but sometimes if you look at the leaderboard and see all their names there you tend to lose your confidence. I mind my own business."

On Saturday, Lehman said: "They don't give a trophy for three rounds. I feel that tomorrow is a good chance for me to put right the things I've learnt over the past few years in major championships, about being patient, being committed, being confident, and just going out and doing it."

On Sunday he did just that, winning the Open at only his third attempt. One cannot emphasise how quickly he has progressed in the past six years. In 1990 he was offered a job as coach of the University of Minnesota golf team. It was tempting to a man who was earning very little money. It offered security of employment and he and Melissa, his wife, were on the point of accepting it when they realised that in the winter when there was little golf instruction to give Lehman would have to rent out skis for cross-country skiing. The Lehmans baulked at that.

"We decided we would give it one more year as a professional golfer," Lehman said. He started to compete on the Nike Tour and had some success. With practically his last remaining money, Lehman travelled to South Africa and entered the South African

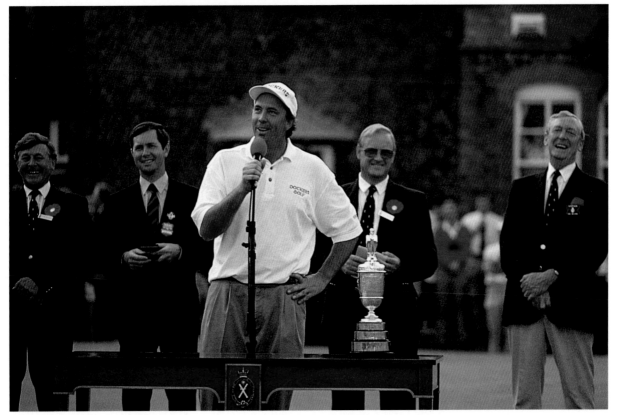

Lehman was gracious and entertaining in his remarks upon receiving the silver claret jug.

Open where he won US$25,000, his biggest payday to date by far. With growing self-confidence, Lehman moved from the Nike Tour to the main PGA Tour and in his first season won US$579,093 and a further US$1,453,905 in the next two years. All this he talked about at Lytham and it came as a reminder of just how far and how fast he had come, enduring the scare of cancer of the colon on the way.

"Up to about 1992 I could not afford to come over here and try to qualify," Lehman said. "Money was tight. We never got around to being flat broke, but we never felt comfortable about going out and splurging it."

There is one other aspect that is most appealing about this 37-year-old man from Minnesota. He is as religious as Steve Jones, as Bernhard Langer, as Paul Azinger, three of his friends. Lehman keeps his beliefs to himself in a way that those who are less religious than he is find gratifying. He does this so successfully he would probably have won over even Earl Weaver, once the manager of baseball's Baltimore Orioles, who would not have a born-again Christian on his team. "When things start turning sour under pressure," Weaver said, "they tell themselves it's God's will."

Lehman returned to the United States on Monday morning and as he did so a story emerged in Britain of something he intended to do that seemed to be another rousing endorsement of him. It appeared that Lehman intended to donate £20,000 to a rehabilitation centre for delinquents in Iowa. "It's a place for delinquents who have reached the end of the rope as far as schooling is concerned. This place is a last chance for them. They are brought in, taught proper values, put back on the right track and returned to society. The school has an 80 per cent success record. Last year I gave £20,000 towards the running costs from my winnings during the season and now I'll be able to send them a cheque for that much from one tournament.

"I support these organizations because I believe it is the biblical thing to do. The Old Testament talks about God getting the first fruits of the harvest. I have been given a gift from God, the benefits of which I feel I should share with others."

And so Lehman flew home leaving behind two impressions: that he was now a golfer of true world class and a genuinely admirable man. There are few of whom the former can be said, even fewer about whom both can be said.

Gary Player (1959, 1968, 1974)

Seve Ballesteros (1979, 1984, 1988)    Bob Charles (1963)

Mark Calcavecchia (1989)    Jack Nicklaus (1966, 1970, 1978)    Sandy Lyle (1985)

RESULTS

# OPEN CHAMPIONSHIP

| YEAR | CHAMPION | SCORE | MARGIN | RUNNERS-UP | VENUE |
|---|---|---|---|---|---|
| 1860 | Willie Park | 174 | 2 | Tom Morris Snr | Prestwick |
| 1861 | Tom Morris Snr | 163 | 4 | Willie Park | Prestwick |
| 1862 | Tom Morris Snr | 163 | 13 | Willie Park | Prestwick |
| 1863 | Willie Park | 168 | 2 | Tom Morris Snr | Prestwick |
| 1864 | Tom Morris Snr | 167 | 2 | Andrew Strath | Prestwick |
| 1865 | Andrew Strath | 162 | 2 | Willie Park | Prestwick |
| 1866 | Willie Park | 169 | 2 | David Park | Prestwick |
| 1867 | Tom Morris Snr | 170 | 2 | Willie Park | Prestwick |
| 1868 | Tom Morris Jnr | 157 | 2 | Robert Andrew | Prestwick |
| 1869 | Tom Morris Jnr | 154 | 3 | Tom Morris Snr | Prestwick |
| 1870 | Tom Morris Jnr | 149 | 12 | Bob Kirk, David Strath | Prestwick |
| 1871 | *No Competition* | | | | |
| 1872 | Tom Morris Jnr | 166 | 3 | David Strath | Prestwick |
| 1873 | Tom Kidd | 179 | 1 | Jamie Anderson | St Andrews |
| 1874 | Mungo Park | 159 | 2 | Tom Morris Jnr | Musselburgh |
| 1875 | Willie Park | 166 | 2 | Bob Martin | Prestwick |
| 1876 | Bob Martin | 176 | — | David Strath | St Andrews |
| | *(Martin was awarded the title when Strath refused to play-off)* | | | | |
| 1877 | Jamie Anderson | 160 | 2 | Bob Pringle | Musselburgh |
| 1878 | Jamie Anderson | 157 | 2 | Bob Kirk | Prestwick |
| 1879 | Jamie Anderson | 169 | 3 | James Allan, Andrew Kirkaldy | St Andrews |
| 1880 | Bob Ferguson | 162 | 5 | Peter Paxton | Musselburgh |
| 1881 | Bob Ferguson | 170 | 3 | Jamie Anderson | Prestwick |
| 1882 | Bob Ferguson | 171 | 3 | Willie Fernie | St Andrews |
| 1883 | Willie Fernie | 159 | Play-off | Bob Ferguson | Musselburgh |
| | *(Fernie won play-off 158 to 159)* | | | | |
| 1884 | Jack Simpson | 160 | 4 | David Rollan, Willie Fernie | Prestwick |
| 1885 | Bob Martin | 171 | 1 | Archie Simpson | St Andrews |
| 1886 | David Brown | 157 | 2 | Willie Campbell | Musselburgh |
| 1887 | Willie Park Jnr | 161 | 1 | Bob Martin | Prestwick |
| 1888 | Jack Burns | 171 | 1 | David Anderson Jnr, Ben Sayers | St Andrews |
| 1889 | Willie Park Jnr | 155 | Play-off | Andrew Kirkaldy | Musselburgh |
| | *(Park won play-off 158 to 163)* | | | | |
| 1890 | *John Ball | 164 | 3 | Willie Fernie, Archie Simpson | Prestwick |
| 1891 | Hugh Kirkaldy | 166 | 2 | Willie Fernie, Andrew Kirkaldy | St Andrews |
| *(From 1892 the competition was extended to 72 holes)* | | | | | |
| 1892 | *Harold Hilton | 305 | 3 | *John Ball Jnr, James Kirkaldy, Sandy Herd | Muirfield |
| 1893 | Willie Auchterlonie | 322 | 2 | *Johnny Laidlay | Prestwick |

| YEAR | CHAMPION | SCORE | MARGIN | RUNNERS-UP | VENUE |
|------|----------|-------|--------|-----------|-------|
| 1894 | J.H. Taylor | 326 | 5 | Douglas Rolland | Sandwich |
| 1895 | J.H. Taylor | 322 | 4 | Sandy Herd | St Andrews |
| 1896 | Harry Vardon | 316 | Play-off | J.H. Taylor | Muirfield |
| | | | | (Vardon won play-off 157 to 161) | |
| 1897 | *Harold H. Hilton | 314 | 1 | James Braid | Hoylake |
| 1898 | Harry Vardon | 307 | 1 | Willie Park | Prestwick |
| 1899 | Harry Vardon | 310 | 5 | Jack White | Sandwich |
| 1900 | J.H. Taylor | 309 | 8 | Harry Vardon | St Andrews |
| 1901 | James Braid | 309 | 3 | Harry Vardon | Muirfield |
| 1902 | Sandy Herd | 307 | 1 | Harry Vardon, James Braid | Hoylake |
| 1903 | Harry Vardon | 300 | 6 | Tom Vardon | Prestwick |
| 1904 | Jack White | 296 | 1 | James Braid, J.H. Taylor | Sandwich |
| 1905 | James Braid | 318 | 5 | J.H. Taylor, R. Jones | St Andrews |
| 1906 | James Braid | 300 | 4 | J.H. Taylor | Muirfield |
| 1907 | Arnaud Massy | 312 | 2 | J.H. Taylor | Hoylake |
| 1908 | James Braid | 291 | 8 | Tom Ball | Prestwick |
| 1909 | J.H. Taylor | 295 | 4 | James Braid | Deal |
| 1910 | James Braid | 299 | 4 | Sandy Herd | St Andrews |
| 1911 | Harry Vardon | 303 | Play-off | Arnaud Massy | Sandwich |
| | | | | (Play-off; Massy conceded at the 35th hole) | |
| 1912 | Ted Ray | 295 | 4 | Harry Vardon | Muirfield |
| 1913 | J.H. Taylor | 304 | 8 | Ted Ray | Hoylake |
| 1914 | Harry Vardon | 306 | 3 | J.H. Taylor | Prestwick |
| *1915-1919 No Championship* | | | | | |
| 1920 | George Duncan | 303 | 2 | Sandy Herd | Deal |
| 1921 | Jock Hutchison | 296 | Play-off | *Roger Wethered | St Andrews |
| | | | | (Hutchison won play-off 150 to 159) | |
| 1922 | Walter Hagen | 300 | 1 | George Duncan, Jim Barnes | Sandwich |
| 1923 | Arthur G. Havers | 295 | 1 | Walter Hagen | Troon |
| 1924 | Walter Hagen | 301 | 1 | Ernest Whitcombe | Hoylake |
| 1925 | Jim Barnes | 300 | 1 | Archie Compston, Ted Ray | Prestwick |
| 1926 | *Robert T. Jones Jnr | 291 | 2 | Al Watrous | Royal Lytham |
| 1927 | *Robert T. Jones Jnr | 285 | 6 | Aubrey Boomer, Fred Robson | St Andrews |
| 1928 | Walter Hagen | 292 | 2 | Gene Sarazen | Sandwich |
| 1929 | Walter Hagen | 292 | 6 | John Farrell | Muirfield |
| 1930 | *Robert T. Jones Jnr | 291 | 2 | Leo Diegel, Macdonald Smith | Hoylake |
| 1931 | Tommy Armour | 296 | 1 | Jose Jurado | Carnoustie |
| 1932 | Gene Sarazen | 283 | 5 | Macdonald Smith | Prince's |
| 1933 | Densmore Shute | 292 | Play-off | Craig Wood | St Andrews |
| | | | | (Shute won play-off 149 to 154) | |
| 1934 | Henry Cotton | 283 | 5 | Sid Brews | Sandwich |
| 1935 | Alf Perry | 283 | 4 | Alf Padgham | Muirfield |
| 1936 | Alf Padgham | 287 | 1 | Jimmy Adams | Hoylake |
| 1937 | Henry Cotton | 290 | 2 | Reg Whitcombe | Carnoustie |
| 1938 | Reg Whitcombe | 295 | 2 | Jimmy Adams | Sandwich |
| 1939 | Richard Burton | 290 | 2 | Johnny Bulla | St Andrews |
| *1940-1945 No Championship* | | | | | |
| 1946 | Sam Snead | 290 | 4 | Bobby Locke, Johnny Bulla | St Andrews |
| 1947 | Fred Daly | 293 | 1 | Reg Horne, *Frank Stranahan | Hoylake |
| 1948 | Henry Cotton | 284 | 5 | Fred Daly | Muirfield |
| 1949 | Bobby Locke | 283 | Play-off | Harry Bradshaw | Sandwich |
| | | | | (Locke won play-off 135 to 147) | |
| 1950 | Bobby Locke | 279 | 2 | Roberto de Vicenzo | Troon |
| 1951 | Max Faulkner | 285 | 2 | Tony Cerda | Royal Portrush |
| 1952 | Bobby Locke | 287 | 1 | Peter Thomson | Royal Lytham |

| YEAR | CHAMPION | SCORE | MARGIN | RUNNERS-UP | VENUE |
|------|----------|-------|--------|------------|-------|
| 1953 | Ben Hogan | 282 | 4 | *Frank Stranahan, Dai Rees, Peter Thomson, Tony Cerda | Carnoustie |
| 1954 | Peter Thomson | 283 | 1 | Sid Scott, Dai Rees, Bobby Locke | Royal Birkdale |
| 1955 | Peter Thomson | 281 | 2 | Johnny Fallon | St Andrews |
| 1956 | Peter Thomson | 286 | 3 | Flory van Donck | Hoylake |
| 1957 | Bobby Locke | 279 | 3 | Peter Thomson | St Andrews |
| 1958 | Peter Thomson | 278 | Play-off | David Thomas (Thomson won play-off 139 to 143) | Royal Lytham |
| 1959 | Gary Player | 284 | 2 | Flory van Donck, Fred Bullock | Muirfield |
| 1960 | Kel Nagle | 278 | 1 | Arnold Palmer | St Andrews |
| 1961 | Arnold Palmer | 284 | 1 | Dai Rees | Royal Birkdale |
| 1962 | Arnold Palmer | 276 | 6 | Kel Nagle | Troon |
| 1963 | Bob Charles | 277 | Play-off | Phil Rodgers (Charles won play-off 140 to 148) | Royal Lytham |
| 1964 | Tony Lema | 279 | 5 | Jack Nicklaus | St Andrews |
| 1965 | Peter Thomson | 285 | 2 | Christy O'Connor, Brian Huggett | Royal Birkdale |
| 1966 | Jack Nicklaus | 282 | 1 | David Thomas, Doug Sanders | Muirfield |
| 1967 | Roberto de Vicenzo | 278 | 2 | Jack Nicklaus | Hoylake |
| 1968 | Gary Player | 289 | 2 | Jack Nicklaus, Bob Charles | Carnoustie |
| 1969 | Tony Jacklin | 280 | 2 | Bob Charles | Royal Lytham |
| 1970 | Jack Nicklaus | 283 | Play-off | Doug Sanders (Nicklaus won play-off 72 to 73) | St Andrews |
| 1971 | Lee Trevino | 278 | 1 | Lu Liang Huan | Royal Birkdale |
| 1972 | Lee Trevino | 278 | 1 | Jack Nicklaus | Muirfield |
| 1973 | Tom Weiskopf | 276 | 3 | Neil Coles, Johnny Miller | Troon |
| 1974 | Gary Player | 282 | 4 | Peter Oosterhuis | Royal Lytham |
| 1975 | Tom Watson | 279 | Play-off | Jack Newton (Watson won play-off 71 to 72) | Carnoustie |
| 1976 | Johnny Miller | 279 | 6 | Jack Nicklaus, Severiano Ballesteros | Royal Birkdale |
| 1977 | Tom Watson | 268 | 1 | Jack Nicklaus | Turnberry |
| 1978 | Jack Nicklaus | 281 | 2 | Simon Owen, Ben Crenshaw, Raymond Floyd, Tom Kite | St Andrews |
| 1979 | Severiano Ballesteros | 283 | 3 | Jack Nicklaus, Ben Crenshaw | Royal Lytham |
| 1980 | Tom Watson | 271 | 4 | Lee Trevino | Muirfield |
| 1981 | Bill Rogers | 276 | 4 | Bernhard Langer | Sandwich |
| 1982 | Tom Watson | 284 | 1 | Peter Oosterhuis, Nick Price | Troon |
| 1983 | Tom Watson | 275 | 1 | Hale Irwin, Andy Bean | Royal Birkdale |
| 1984 | Severiano Ballesteros | 276 | 2 | Bernhard Langer, Tom Watson | St Andrews |
| 1985 | Sandy Lyle | 282 | 1 | Payne Stewart | Sandwich |
| 1986 | Greg Norman | 280 | 5 | Gordon J. Brand | Turnberry |
| 1987 | Nick Faldo | 279 | 1 | Rodger Davis, Paul Azinger | Muirfield |
| 1988 | Severiano Ballesteros | 273 | 2 | Nick Price | Royal Lytham |
| 1989 | Mark Calcavecchia | 275 | Play-off | Greg Norman, Wayne Grady (Calcavecchia won four-hole play-off) | Royal Troon |
| 1990 | Nick Faldo | 270 | 5 | Mark McNulty, Payne Stewart | St Andrews |
| 1991 | Ian Baker-Finch | 272 | 2 | Mike Harwood | Royal Birkdale |
| 1992 | Nick Faldo | 272 | 1 | John Cook | Muirfield |
| 1993 | Greg Norman | 267 | 2 | Nick Faldo | Sandwich |
| 1994 | Nick Price | 268 | 1 | Jesper Parnevik | Turnberry |
| 1995 | John Daly | 282 | Play-off | Costantino Rocca (Daly won four-hole play-off) | St Andrews |
| 1996 | Tom Lehman | 271 | 2 | Mark McCumber, Ernie Els | Royal Lytham |

*Denotes amateurs

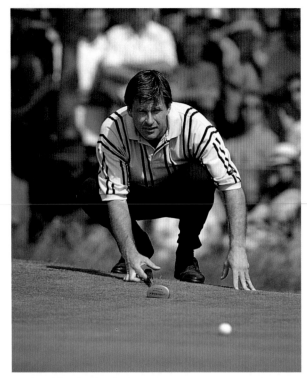

Nick Faldo (1987, 1990, 1992)

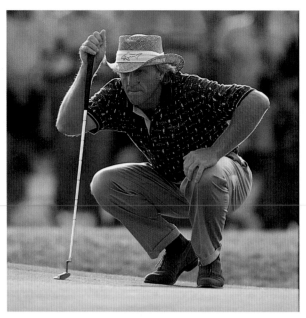

Greg Norman (1986, 1993)

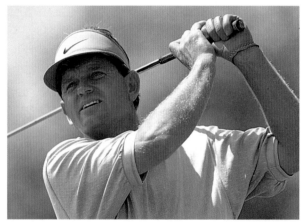

Nick Price (1994)

Ian Baker-Finch (1991)

John Daly (1995)

# OPEN CHAMPIONSHIP

## MOST VICTORIES
**6,** Harry Vardon, 1896-98-99-1903-11-14
**5,** James Braid, 1901-05-06-08-10; J.H. Taylor, 1894-95-1900-09-13; Peter Thomson, 1954-55-56-58-65; Tom Watson, 1975-77-80-82-83

## MOST TIMES RUNNER-UP OR JOINT RUNNER-UP
**7,** Jack Nicklaus, 1964-67-68-72-76-77-79
**6,** J.H. Taylor, 1896-1904-05-06-07-14

## OLDEST WINNER
Old Tom Morris, 46 years 99 days, 1867
Roberto de Vicenzo, 44 years 93 days, 1967

## YOUNGEST WINNER
Young Tom Morris, 17 years 5 months 8 days, 1868
Willie Auchterlonie, 21 years 24 days, 1893
Severiano Ballesteros, 22 years 3 months 12 days, 1979

## YOUNGEST AND OLDEST COMPETITOR
John Ball, 14 years, 1878
Gene Sarazen, 71 years 4 months 13 days, 1973

## BIGGEST MARGIN OF VICTORY
**13** strokes, Old Tom Morris, 1862
**12** strokes, Young Tom Morris, 1870
**8** strokes, J.H. Taylor, 1900 and 1913; James Braid, 1908
**6** strokes, Bobby Jones, 1927; Walter Hagen, 1929; Arnold Palmer, 1962; Johnny Miller, 1976

## LOWEST WINNING AGGREGATES
**267** (66, 68, 69, 64), Greg Norman, Royal St George's, 1993
**268** (68, 70, 65, 65), Tom Watson, Turnberry, 1977; (69, 66, 67, 66), Nick Price, Turnberry, 1994
**270** (67, 65, 67, 71), Nick Faldo, St Andrews, 1990
**271** (68, 70, 64, 69), Tom Watson, Muirfield, 1980; (67, 67, 64, 73), Tom Lehman, Royal Lytham, 1996

## LOWEST AGGREGATES BY RUNNER-UP
**269** (68, 70, 65, 66), Jack Nicklaus, Turnberry, 1977; (69, 63, 70, 67), Nick Faldo, Royal St George's, 1993; (68, 66, 68, 67), Jesper Parnevik, Turnberry, 1994
**273** (66, 67, 70, 70), John Cook, Muirfield, 1992; (67, 69, 71, 66), Mark McCumber, and (68, 67, 71, 67), Ernie Els, Royal Lytham, 1996

## LOWEST AGGREGATE BY AN AMATEUR
**281** (68, 72, 70, 71), Iain Pyman, Royal St George's, 1993; (75, 66, 70, 70), Tiger Woods, Royal Lytham, 1996

## LOWEST INDIVIDUAL ROUND
**63,** Mark Hayes, second round, Turnberry, 1977; Isao Aoki, third round, Muirfield, 1980; Greg Norman, second round, Turnberry, 1986; Paul Broadhurst, third round, St Andrews, 1990; Jodie Mudd, fourth round, Royal Birkdale, 1991; Nick Faldo, second round, and Payne Stewart, fourth round, Royal St George's, 1993

## LOWEST INDIVIDUAL ROUND BY AN AMATEUR
**66,** Frank Stranahan, fourth round, Troon, 1950; Tiger Woods, second round, Royal Lytham, 1996

## LOWEST FIRST ROUND
**64,** Craig Stadler, Royal Birkdale, 1983; Christy O'Connor Jr., Royal St George's, 1985; Rodger Davis, Muirfield, 1987; Raymond Floyd and Steve Pate, Muirfield, 1992

## LOWEST SECOND ROUND
**63,** Mark Hayes, Turnberry, 1977; Greg Norman, Turnberry, 1986; Nick Faldo, Royal St George's, 1993

## LOWEST THIRD ROUND
**63,** Isao Aoki, Muirfield, 1980; Paul Broadhurst, St Andrews, 1990

## LOWEST FOURTH ROUND
**63,** Jodie Mudd, Royal Birkdale, 1991; Payne Stewart, Royal St George's, 1993

## LOWEST FIRST 36 HOLES
**130** (66, 64), Nick Faldo, Muirfield, 1992

## LOWEST SECOND 36 HOLES
**130** (65, 65), Tom Watson, Turnberry, 1977; (64, 66), Ian Baker-Finch, Royal Birkdale, 1991; (66, 64), Anders Forsbrand, Turnberry, 1994

## LOWEST FIRST 54 HOLES
**198** (67, 67, 64), Tom Lehman, Royal Lytham, 1996

## LOWEST FINAL 54 HOLES
**199** (66, 67, 66), Nick Price, Turnberry, 1994

## LOWEST 9 HOLES
28, Denis Durnian, first 9, Royal Birkdale, 1983
29, Peter Thomson and Tom Haliburton, first 9, Royal Lytham, 1958; Tony Jacklin, first 9, St Andrews, 1970; Bill Longmuir, first 9, Royal Lytham, 1979; David J. Russell, first 9, Royal Lytham, 1988; Ian Baker-Finch and Paul Broadhurst, first 9, St Andrews, 1990; Ian Baker-Finch, first 9, Royal Birkdale, 1991; Paul McGinley, first 9, Royal Lytham, 1996

## CHAMPIONS IN THREE DECADES
Harry Vardon, 1896, 1903, 1911
J.H. Taylor, 1894, 1900, 1913
Gary Player, 1959, 1968, 1974

## BIGGEST SPAN BETWEEN FIRST AND LAST VICTORIES
19 years, J.H. Taylor, 1894-1913
18 years, Harry Vardon, 1896-1914
15 years, Gary Player, 1959-74
14 years, Henry Cotton, 1934-48

## SUCCESSIVE VICTORIES
4, Young Tom Morris, 1868-72. No championship in 1871
3, Jamie Anderson, 1877-79; Bob Ferguson, 1880-82, Peter Thomson, 1954-56
2, Old Tom Morris, 1861-62; J.H. Taylor, 1894-95; Harry Vardon, 1898-99; James Braid, 1905-06; Bobby Jones, 1926-27; Walter Hagen, 1928-29; Bobby Locke, 1949-50; Arnold Palmer, 1961-62; Lee Trevino, 1971-72; Tom Watson, 1982-83

## VICTORIES BY AMATEURS
3, Bobby Jones, 1926-27-30
2, Harold Hilton, 1892-97
1, John Ball, 1890
Roger Wethered lost a play-off in 1921

## HIGHEST NUMBER OF TOP FIVE FINISHES
16, J.H. Taylor, Jack Nicklaus
15, Harry Vardon, James Braid

## HIGHEST NUMBER OF ROUNDS UNDER 70
33, Jack Nicklaus, Nick Faldo
27, Tom Watson
22, Greg Norman
21, Lee Trevino
20, Severiano Ballesteros

## OUTRIGHT LEADER AFTER EVERY ROUND
Willie Auchterlonie, 1893; J.H. Taylor, 1894 and 1900; James Braid, 1908; Ted Ray, 1912; Bobby Jones, 1927; Gene Sarazen, 1932; Henry Cotton, 1934; Tom Weiskopf, 1973

## RECORD LEADS (SINCE 1892)
**After 18 holes:**
4 strokes, James Braid, 1908; Bobby Jones, 1927; Henry Cotton, 1934; Christy O'Connor Jr., 1985
**After 36 holes:**
9 strokes, Henry Cotton, 1934
**After 54 holes:**
10 strokes, Henry Cotton, 1934

7 strokes, Tony Lema, 1964
6 strokes, James Braid, 1908; Tom Lehman, 1996

## CHAMPIONS WITH EACH ROUND LOWER THAN PREVIOUS ONE
Jack White, 1904, Sandwich, (80, 75, 72, 69)
James Braid, 1906, Muirfield, (77, 76, 74, 73)
Ben Hogan, 1953, Carnoustie, (73, 71, 70, 68)
Gary Player, 1959, Muirfield, (75, 71, 70, 68)

## CHAMPION WITH FOUR ROUNDS THE SAME
Densmore Shute, 1933, St Andrews, (73, 73, 73, 73) (excluding the play-off)

## BIGGEST VARIATION BETWEEN ROUNDS OF A CHAMPION
14 strokes, Henry Cotton, 1934, second round 65, fourth round 79
11 strokes, Jack White, 1904, first round 80, fourth round 69; Greg Norman, 1986, first round 74, second round 63, third round 74

## BIGGEST VARIATION BETWEEN TWO ROUNDS
17 strokes, Jack Nicklaus, 1981, first round 83, second round 66; Ian Baker-Finch, 1986, first round 86, second round 69

## BEST COMEBACK BY CHAMPIONS
**After 18 holes:**
Harry Vardon, 1896, 11 strokes behind the leader
**After 36 holes:**
George Duncan, 1920, 13 strokes behind the leader
**After 54 holes:**
Jim Barnes, 1925, 5 strokes behind the leader
Tommy Armour, 1931, 5 strokes behind the leader
Of non-champions, Greg Norman, 1989, 7 strokes behind the leader and lost in a play-off

## CHAMPIONS WITH FOUR ROUNDS UNDER 70
Greg Norman, 1993, Royal St George's, (66, 68, 69, 64); Nick Price, 1994, Turnberry, (69, 66, 67, 66)
**Of non-champions:**
Ernie Els, 1993, Royal St George's, (68, 69, 69, 68); Jesper Parnevik, 1994, Turnberry, (68, 66, 68, 67)

## BEST FINISHING ROUND BY A CHAMPION
64, Greg Norman, Royal St George's, 1993
65, Tom Watson, Turnberry, 1977; Severiano Ballesteros, Royal Lytham, 1988
66, Johnny Miller, Royal Birkdale, 1976; Ian Baker-Finch, Royal Birkdale, 1991; Nick Price, Turnberry, 1994

## WORST FINISHING ROUND BY A CHAMPION SINCE 1920
79, Henry Cotton, Sandwich, 1934
78, Reg Whitcombe, Sandwich, 1938
77, Walter Hagen, Hoylake, 1924

## WORST OPENING ROUND BY A CHAMPION SINCE 1919
80, George Duncan, Deal, 1920 (he also had a second round of 80)
77, Walter Hagen, Hoylake, 1924

## BEST OPENING ROUND BY A CHAMPION

**66,** Peter Thomson, Royal Lytham, 1958; Nick Faldo, Muirfield, 1992; Greg Norman, Royal St George's, 1993
**67,** Henry Cotton, Sandwich, 1934; Tom Watson, Royal Birkdale, 1983; Severiano Ballesteros, Royal Lytham, 1988; Nick Faldo, St Andrews, 1990; John Daly, St Andrews, 1995; Tom Lehman, Royal Lytham, 1996

## BIGGEST RECOVERY IN 18 HOLES BY A CHAMPION

George Duncan, Deal, 1920, was 13 strokes behind the leader, Abe Mitchell, after 36 holes and level after 54

## MOST APPEARANCES ON FINAL DAY (SINCE 1892)

**31,** Jack Nicklaus
**30,** J.H. Taylor
**27,** Harry Vardon, James Braid
**26,** Peter Thomson, Gary Player
**23,** Dai Rees
**22,** Henry Cotton

## CHAMPIONSHIP WITH HIGHEST NUMBER OF ROUNDS UNDER 70

**148,** Turnberry, 1994

## CHAMPIONSHIP SINCE 1946 WITH THE FEWEST ROUNDS UNDER 70

St Andrews, 1946; Hoylake, 1947; Portrush, 1951; Hoylake, 1956; Carnoustie, 1968. All had only two rounds under 70

## LONGEST COURSE

Carnoustie, 1968, 7252 yd (6631 m)

## COURSES MOST OFTEN USED

St Andrews, 25; Prestwick, 24; Muirfield, 14; Sandwich, 12; Hoylake, 10; Royal Lytham, 9; Royal Birkdale, 7; Musselburgh, and Royal Troon, 6; Carnoustie, 5; Turnberry, 3; Deal, 2; Royal Portrush and Prince's, 1

## PRIZE MONEY

| Year | Total | First Prize |
|---|---|---|
| 1860 | nil | nil |
| 1863 | 10 | nil |
| 1864 | 16 | 6 |
| 1876 | 27 | 10 |
| 1889 | 22 | 8 |
| 1891 | 28.50 | 10 |
| 1892 | 110 | (Amateur winner) |
| 1893 | 100 | 30 |
| 1910 | 125 | 50 |
| 1920 | 225 | 75 |
| 1927 | 275 | 100 |
| 1930 | 400 | 100 |
| 1931 | 500 | 100 |
| 1946 | 1,000 | 150 |
| 1949 | 1,700 | 300 |
| 1953 | 2,450 | 500 |
| 1954 | 3,500 | 750 |
| 1955 | 3,750 | 1,000 |
| 1958 | 4,850 | 1,000 |
| 1959 | 5,000 | 1,000 |
| 1960 | 7,000 | 1,250 |
| 1961 | 8,500 | 1,400 |
| 1963 | 8,500 | 1,500 |
| 1965 | 10,000 | 1,750 |
| 1966 | 15,000 | 2,100 |
| 1968 | 20,000 | 3,000 |
| 1969 | 30,000 | 4,250 |
| 1970 | 40,000 | 5,250 |
| 1971 | 45,000 | 5,500 |
| 1972 | 50,000 | 5,500 |
| 1975 | 75,000 | 7,500 |
| 1977 | 100,000 | 10,000 |
| 1978 | 125,000 | 12,500 |
| 1979 | 155,000 | 15,500 |
| 1980 | 200,000 | 25,000 |
| 1982 | 250,000 | 32,000 |
| 1983 | 300,000 | 40,000 |
| 1984 | 451,000 | 55,000 |
| 1985 | 530,000 | 65,000 |
| 1986 | 600,000 | 70,000 |
| 1987 | 650,000 | 75,000 |
| 1988 | 700,000 | 80,000 |
| 1989 | 750,000 | 80,000 |
| 1990 | 825,000 | 85,000 |
| 1991 | 900,000 | 90,000 |
| 1992 | 950,000 | 95,000 |
| 1993 | 1,000,000 | 100,000 |
| 1994 | 1,100,000 | 110,000 |
| 1995 | 1,250,000 | 125,000 |
| 1996 | 1,400,000 | 200,000 |

## ATTENDANCE

| Year | Attendance |
|---|---|
| 1962 | 37,098 |
| 1963 | 24,585 |
| 1964 | 35,954 |
| 1965 | 32,927 |
| 1966 | 40,182 |
| 1967 | 29,880 |
| 1968 | 51,819 |
| 1969 | 46,001 |
| 1970 | 81,593 |
| 1971 | 70,076 |
| 1972 | 84,746 |
| 1973 | 78,810 |
| 1974 | 92,796 |
| 1975 | 85,258 |
| 1976 | 92,021 |
| 1977 | 87,615 |
| 1978 | 125,271 |
| 1979 | 134,501 |
| 1980 | 131,610 |
| 1981 | 111,987 |
| 1982 | 133,299 |
| 1983 | 142,892 |
| 1984 | 193,126 |
| 1985 | 141,619 |
| 1986 | 134,261 |
| 1987 | 139,189 |
| 1988 | 191,334 |
| 1989 | 160,639 |
| 1990 | 208,680 |
| 1991 | 189,435 |
| 1992 | 146,427 |
| 1993 | 141,000 |
| 1994 | 128,000 |
| 1995 | 180,000 |
| 1996 | 170,000 |

COMPLETE SCORES

# 125TH OPEN CHAMPIONSHIP

*Denotes amateurs

| HOLE | | 1 | 2 | 3 | 4 | 5 | 6 | 7 | 8 | 9 | 10 | 11 | 12 | 13 | 14 | 15 | 16 | 17 | 18 | |
|---|---|---|---|---|---|---|---|---|---|---|---|---|---|---|---|---|---|---|---|---|
| PAR | | 3 | 4 | 4 | 4 | 3 | 5 | 5 | 4 | 3 | 4 | 5 | 3 | 4 | 4 | 4 | 4 | 4 | 4 | TOTAL |
| **Tom Lehman** | Round 1 | 3 | 4 | 4 | 3 | 2 | 4 | 5 | 4 | 3 | 4 | 5 | 3 | 6 | 3 | 4 | 3 | 3 | 4 | 67 |
| USA | Round 2 | 4 | 3 | 4 | 4 | 3 | 4 | 4 | 4 | 3 | 4 | 5 | 3 | 3 | 4 | 4 | 4 | 3 | 4 | 67 |
| £200,000 | Round 3 | 2 | 3 | 4 | 3 | 3 | 4 | 5 | 4 | 2 | 4 | 4 | 3 | 4 | 3 | 4 | 3 | 4 | 5 | 64 |
| | Round 4 | 3 | 4 | 5 | 4 | 3 | 5 | 5 | 4 | 3 | 4 | 5 | 2 | 4 | 5 | 4 | 4 | 5 | 4 | 73-271 |
| **Mark McCumber** | Round 1 | 3 | 4 | 5 | 3 | 2 | 4 | 4 | 4 | 3 | 4 | 5 | 3 | 3 | 4 | 5 | 4 | 3 | 4 | 67 |
| USA | Round 2 | 3 | 3 | 4 | 4 | 2 | 4 | 5 | 4 | 3 | 4 | 4 | 2 | 5 | 5 | 4 | 3 | 5 | 5 | 69 |
| £125,000 | Round 3 | 3 | 3 | 4 | 4 | 4 | 4 | 6 | 4 | 2 | 4 | 5 | 3 | 4 | 5 | 4 | 4 | 4 | 4 | 71 |
| | Round 4 | 3 | 4 | 4 | 4 | 3 | 4 | 4 | 3 | 3 | 4 | 4 | 3 | 4 | 3 | 5 | 3 | 4 | 4 | 66-273 |
| **Ernie Els** | Round 1 | 3 | 4 | 4 | 4 | 3 | 4 | 5 | 3 | 3 | 4 | 5 | 3 | 4 | 4 | 3 | 3 | 4 | 5 | 68 |
| South Africa | Round 2 | 4 | 3 | 4 | 4 | 3 | 5 | 3 | 4 | 3 | 3 | 5 | 3 | 4 | 3 | 5 | 4 | 4 | 3 | 67 |
| £125,000 | Round 3 | 4 | 4 | 5 | 5 | 3 | 4 | 4 | 4 | 2 | 4 | 5 | 2 | 4 | 5 | 4 | 3 | 5 | 4 | 71 |
| | Round 4 | 3 | 3 | 5 | 4 | 3 | 4 | 4 | 4 | 3 | 3 | 5 | 2 | 3 | 4 | 3 | 5 | 4 | 5 | 67-273 |
| **Nick Faldo** | Round 1 | 4 | 4 | 4 | 4 | 3 | 4 | 5 | 4 | 3 | 4 | 4 | 3 | 4 | 4 | 3 | 4 | 4 | 3 | 68 |
| England | Round 2 | 3 | 4 | 4 | 3 | 3 | 5 | 4 | 4 | 3 | 3 | 5 | 4 | 4 | 4 | 4 | 3 | 4 | 4 | 68 |
| £75,000 | Round 3 | 3 | 4 | 4 | 5 | 3 | 3 | 4 | 3 | 3 | 4 | 4 | 3 | 4 | 5 | 4 | 5 | 3 | 4 | 68 |
| | Round 4 | 3 | 4 | 4 | 3 | 3 | 5 | 5 | 4 | 2 | 4 | 5 | 3 | 4 | 4 | 5 | 4 | 4 | 4 | 70-274 |
| **Jeff Maggert** | Round 1 | 3 | 4 | 4 | 3 | 4 | 6 | 4 | 4 | 3 | 4 | 4 | 3 | 4 | 4 | 4 | 4 | 3 | 4 | 69 |
| USA | Round 2 | 3 | 4 | 4 | 3 | 3 | 4 | 4 | 4 | 3 | 4 | 5 | 4 | 5 | 3 | 5 | 4 | 4 | 4 | 70 |
| £50,000 | Round 3 | 3 | 4 | 5 | 4 | 3 | 5 | 5 | 5 | 3 | 4 | 3 | 3 | 3 | 4 | 4 | 4 | 5 | 4 | 72 |
| | Round 4 | 2 | 3 | 4 | 4 | 3 | 5 | 4 | 3 | 4 | 4 | 4 | 3 | 2 | 5 | 4 | 3 | 4 | 4 | 65-276 |
| **Mark Brooks** | Round 1 | 3 | 4 | 4 | 3 | 4 | 4 | 3 | 4 | 3 | 3 | 4 | 4 | 3 | 4 | 5 | 4 | 4 | 4 | 67 |
| USA | Round 2 | 4 | 4 | 4 | 4 | 3 | 4 | 5 | 3 | 3 | 4 | 4 | 4 | 4 | 4 | 4 | 4 | 4 | 4 | 70 |
| £50,000 | Round 3 | 3 | 4 | 4 | 4 | 3 | 4 | 5 | 3 | 3 | 4 | 3 | 3 | 4 | 4 | 4 | 4 | 4 | 4 | 68 |
| | Round 4 | 3 | 3 | 4 | 3 | 3 | 4 | 5 | 5 | 3 | 4 | 5 | 3 | 4 | 4 | 4 | 5 | 5 | | 71-276 |
| **Peter Hedblom** | Round 1 | 3 | 3 | 4 | 4 | 3 | 5 | 5 | 5 | 3 | 5 | 6 | 4 | 3 | 3 | 4 | 4 | 3 | 4 | 70 |
| Sweden | Round 2 | 4 | 3 | 4 | 5 | 3 | 4 | 4 | 4 | 3 | 3 | 4 | 3 | 4 | 3 | 4 | 3 | 3 | 4 | 65 |
| £35,000 | Round 3 | 2 | 3 | 4 | 4 | 3 | 4 | 4 | 5 | 3 | 4 | 6 | 4 | 4 | 7 | 4 | 4 | 6 | 4 | 75 |
| | Round 4 | 3 | 4 | 4 | 4 | 2 | 3 | 5 | 4 | 3 | 4 | 5 | 3 | 3 | 4 | 5 | 3 | 4 | 4 | 67-277 |
| **Greg Norman** | Round 1 | 3 | 4 | 5 | 4 | 3 | 3 | 6 | 4 | 3 | 4 | 4 | 3 | 4 | 4 | 4 | 4 | 5 | 4 | 71 |
| Australia | Round 2 | 3 | 5 | 5 | 4 | 4 | 5 | 4 | 3 | 2 | 4 | 3 | 3 | 3 | 4 | 4 | 5 | 4 | 3 | 68 |
| £35,000 | Round 3 | 3 | 4 | 4 | 3 | 4 | 4 | 4 | 4 | 2 | 4 | 5 | 3 | 4 | 5 | 4 | 5 | 4 | 5 | 71 |
| | Round 4 | 4 | 3 | 3 | 4 | 4 | 4 | 3 | 4 | 2 | 4 | 4 | 3 | 4 | 5 | 5 | 4 | 3 | 4 | 67-277 |

| HOLE | | 1 | 2 | 3 | 4 | 5 | 6 | 7 | 8 | 9 | 10 | 11 | 12 | 13 | 14 | 15 | 16 | 17 | 18 | |
|---|---|---|---|---|---|---|---|---|---|---|---|---|---|---|---|---|---|---|---|---|
| PAR | | 3 | 4 | 4 | 4 | 3 | 5 | 5 | 4 | 3 | 4 | 5 | 3 | 4 | 4 | 4 | 4 | 4 | 4 | TOTAL |
| **Greg Turner** | Round 1 | 2 | 3 | 4 | 5 | 3 | 5 | 5 | 4 | 3 | 4 | 4 | 4 | 3 | 4 | 4 | 6 | 5 | 4 | 72 |
| New Zealand | Round 2 | 3 | 4 | 3 | 3 | 3 | 5 | 5 | 4 | 3 | 3 | 5 | 3 | 4 | 4 | 4 | 4 | 5 | 4 | 69 |
| £35,000 | Round 3 | 2 | 3 | 5 | 4 | 4 | 5 | 4 | 4 | 3 | 4 | 5 | 3 | 4 | 4 | 4 | 3 | 4 | 3 | 68 |
| | Round 4 | 3 | 5 | 3 | 4 | 3 | 4 | 5 | 5 | 2 | 4 | 4 | 3 | 3 | 4 | 3 | 4 | 4 | 5 | 68-277 |
| **Fred Couples** | Round 1 | 3 | 4 | 4 | 3 | 2 | 5 | 4 | 4 | 3 | 3 | 4 | 3 | 5 | 4 | 4 | 4 | 4 | 4 | 67 |
| USA | Round 2 | 3 | 5 | 4 | 5 | 4 | 4 | 3 | 3 | 3 | 3 | 5 | 3 | 3 | 4 | 5 | 4 | 5 | 4 | 70 |
| £35,000 | Round 3 | 3 | 4 | 4 | 4 | 3 | 4 | 5 | 3 | 2 | 4 | 5 | 3 | 5 | 4 | 4 | 4 | 4 | 4 | 69 |
| | Round 4 | 2 | 4 | 4 | 3 | 2 | 4 | 5 | 4 | 2 | 5 | 6 | 3 | 5 | 4 | 4 | 4 | 5 | 5 | 71-277 |
| **Alexander Cejka** | Round 1 | 4 | 5 | 4 | 4 | 3 | 4 | 4 | 5 | 3 | 4 | 4 | 3 | 5 | 4 | 5 | 4 | 4 | 4 | 73 |
| Germany | Round 2 | 3 | 4 | 3 | 4 | 3 | 7 | 4 | 3 | 2 | 4 | 5 | 3 | 3 | 4 | 4 | 3 | 4 | 4 | 67 |
| £27,000 | Round 3 | 2 | 4 | 4 | 4 | 3 | 5 | 6 | 3 | 3 | 4 | 4 | 4 | 4 | 3 | 4 | 3 | 5 | 6 | 71 |
| | Round 4 | 2 | 4 | 4 | 4 | 3 | 4 | 4 | 4 | 3 | 4 | 5 | 3 | 4 | 5 | 4 | 3 | 3 | 4 | 67-278 |
| **Darren Clarke** | Round 1 | 3 | 4 | 5 | 4 | 3 | 5 | 4 | 4 | 3 | 5 | 4 | 3 | 4 | 4 | 3 | 4 | 4 | 4 | 70 |
| N. Ireland | Round 2 | 3 | 4 | 3 | 3 | 3 | 5 | 4 | 4 | 3 | 5 | 4 | 3 | 4 | 4 | 5 | 4 | 3 | 4 | 68 |
| £27,000 | Round 3 | 2 | 5 | 4 | 4 | 3 | 5 | 3 | 4 | 3 | 4 | 4 | 3 | 4 | 4 | 4 | 4 | 4 | 5 | 69 |
| | Round 4 | 3 | 4 | 4 | 4 | 4 | 4 | 5 | 4 | 3 | 5 | 5 | 3 | 3 | 4 | 3 | 4 | 4 | 5 | 71-278 |
| **Vijay Singh** | Round 1 | 3 | 4 | 3 | 5 | 4 | 5 | 4 | 4 | 3 | 3 | 4 | 3 | 4 | 4 | 4 | 4 | 4 | 4 | 69 |
| Fiji | Round 2 | 3 | 4 | 5 | 3 | 3 | 5 | 4 | 3 | 3 | 4 | 4 | 3 | 4 | 4 | 4 | 3 | 5 | 3 | 67 |
| £27,000 | Round 3 | 3 | 5 | 3 | 4 | 2 | 4 | 5 | 5 | 3 | 4 | 4 | 4 | 4 | 5 | 4 | 4 | 3 | 3 | 69 |
| | Round 4 | 3 | 4 | 4 | 4 | 3 | 6 | 4 | 4 | 3 | 5 | 5 | 3 | 4 | 4 | 4 | 4 | 5 | 4 | 73-278 |
| **Mark McNulty** | Round 1 | 3 | 4 | 4 | 4 | 3 | 5 | 3 | 4 | 3 | 3 | 5 | 2 | 4 | 5 | 5 | 4 | 4 | 4 | 69 |
| Zimbabwe | Round 2 | 3 | 4 | 5 | 5 | 4 | 4 | 4 | 5 | 3 | 3 | 4 | 3 | 3 | 4 | 5 | 3 | 5 | 4 | 71 |
| £20,250 | Round 3 | 3 | 3 | 3 | 4 | 3 | 4 | 5 | 4 | 3 | 4 | 4 | 3 | 4 | 5 | 5 | 5 | 4 | 4 | 70 |
| | Round 4 | 3 | 4 | 5 | 5 | 3 | 3 | 4 | 4 | 3 | 4 | 5 | 3 | 4 | 4 | 4 | 4 | 4 | 3 | 69-279 |
| **David Duval** | Round 1 | 3 | 4 | 5 | 4 | 3 | 4 | 5 | 4 | 3 | 4 | 4 | 5 | 4 | 5 | 4 | 4 | 6 | 4 | 76 |
| USA | Round 2 | 3 | 4 | 5 | 3 | 2 | 5 | 4 | 4 | 2 | 3 | 6 | 3 | 4 | 4 | 3 | 3 | 4 | 5 | 67 |
| £20,250 | Round 3 | 3 | 4 | 4 | 5 | 3 | 4 | 5 | 3 | 3 | 4 | 5 | 2 | 3 | 4 | 4 | 4 | 4 | 3 | 66 |
| | Round 4 | 3 | 4 | 5 | 4 | 4 | 3 | 4 | 4 | 3 | 4 | 5 | 3 | 5 | 4 | 4 | 3 | 4 | 4 | 70-279 |
| **Paul McGinley** | Round 1 | 3 | 4 | 4 | 4 | 4 | 4 | 4 | 5 | 3 | 3 | 5 | 3 | 3 | 4 | 5 | 3 | 4 | 4 | 69 |
| Ireland | Round 2 | 2 | 4 | 4 | 3 | 3 | 5 | 4 | 3 | 1 | 4 | 5 | 3 | 4 | 3 | 5 | 4 | 3 | 5 | 65 |
| £20,250 | Round 3 | 4 | 4 | 4 | 3 | 5 | 5 | 4 | 4 | 4 | 3 | 5 | 4 | 4 | 5 | 4 | 4 | 4 | 4 | 74 |
| | Round 4 | 3 | 4 | 4 | 5 | 3 | 4 | 4 | 4 | 2 | 4 | 5 | 3 | 4 | 4 | 4 | 4 | 5 | 5 | 71-279 |
| **Shigeki Maruyama** | Round 1 | 3 | 4 | 4 | 4 | 3 | 3 | 4 | 4 | 3 | 4 | 5 | 3 | 3 | 4 | 6 | 3 | 4 | 4 | 68 |
| Japan | Round 2 | 3 | 4 | 5 | 3 | 3 | 5 | 4 | 4 | 3 | 4 | 6 | 3 | 3 | 4 | 5 | 3 | 5 | 3 | 70 |
| £20,250 | Round 3 | 3 | 4 | 5 | 3 | 3 | 4 | 4 | 5 | 3 | 3 | 4 | 3 | 4 | 4 | 4 | 4 | 4 | 5 | 69 |
| | Round 4 | 3 | 4 | 4 | 4 | 2 | 7 | 4 | 4 | 3 | 4 | 4 | 3 | 4 | 5 | 5 | 4 | 4 | 4 | 72-279 |
| **Michael Welch** | Round 1 | 3 | 3 | 4 | 4 | 4 | 4 | 4 | 6 | 3 | 4 | 4 | 3 | 4 | 4 | 4 | 3 | 6 | 4 | 71 |
| England | Round 2 | 4 | 5 | 3 | 4 | 3 | 4 | 4 | 3 | 2 | 4 | 4 | 4 | 3 | 4 | 4 | 5 | 4 | 4 | 68 |
| £15,500 | Round 3 | 3 | 3 | 5 | 4 | 3 | 4 | 4 | 4 | 3 | 4 | 6 | 4 | 5 | 4 | 4 | 4 | 4 | 5 | 73 |
| | Round 4 | 4 | 4 | 4 | 4 | 3 | 4 | 4 | 4 | 3 | 4 | 5 | 4 | 3 | 3 | 3 | 3 | 4 | 5 | 68-280 |
| **Padraig Harrington** | Round 1 | 4 | 4 | 4 | 4 | 3 | 5 | 4 | 4 | 3 | 4 | 4 | 2 | 4 | 4 | 4 | 3 | 4 | 4 | 68 |
| Ireland | Round 2 | 3 | 4 | 4 | 4 | 3 | 4 | 5 | 5 | 2 | 4 | 5 | 2 | 5 | 4 | 4 | 4 | 3 | 3 | 68 |
| £15,500 | Round 3 | 3 | 4 | 4 | 4 | 4 | 5 | 4 | 4 | 3 | 4 | 5 | 3 | 4 | 4 | 4 | 4 | 6 | 4 | 73 |
| | Round 4 | 3 | 4 | 5 | 4 | 3 | 4 | 4 | 4 | 3 | 4 | 5 | 2 | 3 | 4 | 5 | 5 | 4 | 5 | 71-280 |
| **Loren Roberts** | Round 1 | 2 | 4 | 4 | 3 | 2 | 5 | 4 | 5 | 3 | 3 | 5 | 2 | 4 | 4 | 5 | 4 | 3 | 5 | 67 |
| USA | Round 2 | 3 | 4 | 4 | 4 | 3 | 4 | 5 | 5 | 3 | 4 | 5 | 3 | 4 | 4 | 4 | 3 | 4 | 3 | 69 |
| £15,500 | Round 3 | 3 | 5 | 4 | 4 | 4 | 4 | 5 | 5 | 3 | 4 | 5 | 3 | 3 | 3 | 4 | 4 | 5 | 4 | 72 |
| | Round 4 | 3 | 4 | 4 | 4 | 3 | 4 | 5 | 4 | 3 | 5 | 4 | 4 | 3 | 5 | 4 | 5 | 4 | 4 | 72-280 |

| HOLE | | 1 | 2 | 3 | 4 | 5 | 6 | 7 | 8 | 9 | 10 | 11 | 12 | 13 | 14 | 15 | 16 | 17 | 18 | |
|---|---|---|---|---|---|---|---|---|---|---|---|---|---|---|---|---|---|---|---|---|
| PAR | | 3 | 4 | 4 | 4 | 3 | 5 | 5 | 4 | 3 | 4 | 5 | 3 | 4 | 4 | 4 | 4 | 4 | 4 | TOTAL |
| **Rocco Mediate** | Round 1 | 3 | 3 | 4 | 4 | 2 | 5 | 5 | 4 | 3 | 4 | 4 | 3 | 4 | 4 | 5 | 4 | 4 | 4 | 69 |
| USA | Round 2 | 4 | 4 | 6 | 4 | 4 | 4 | 4 | 3 | 3 | 5 | 4 | 3 | 4 | 3 | 4 | 3 | 4 | 4 | 70 |
| £15,500 | Round 3 | 3 | 4 | 3 | 6 | 2 | 4 | 5 | 5 | 3 | 4 | 4 | 3 | 4 | 4 | 4 | 4 | 3 | 4 | 69 |
| | Round 4 | 3 | 4 | 6 | 4 | 3 | 4 | 5 | 4 | 3 | 4 | 5 | 3 | 3 | 5 | 4 | 4 | 4 | 4 | 72-280 |
| **Mark James** | Round 1 | 3 | 4 | 4 | 4 | 3 | 4 | 5 | 4 | 3 | 4 | 4 | 3 | 4 | 4 | 5 | 4 | 4 | 4 | 70 |
| England | Round 2 | 3 | 3 | 5 | 3 | 3 | 5 | 4 | 4 | 3 | 3 | 4 | 2 | 4 | 5 | 4 | 4 | 4 | 5 | 68 |
| £11,875 | Round 3 | 3 | 4 | 4 | 4 | 3 | 5 | 5 | 3 | 3 | 4 | 6 | 4 | 3 | 4 | 5 | 5 | 6 | 4 | 75 |
| | Round 4 | 3 | 4 | 5 | 3 | 3 | 5 | 5 | 4 | 3 | 4 | 4 | 3 | 3 | 4 | 4 | 4 | 3 | 4 | 68-281 |
| **Jay Haas** | Round 1 | 3 | 4 | 4 | 4 | 3 | 4 | 4 | 5 | 3 | 4 | 4 | 3 | 4 | 4 | 4 | 4 | 4 | 5 | 70 |
| USA | Round 2 | 3 | 4 | 5 | 4 | 3 | 5 | 4 | 3 | 5 | 4 | 5 | 3 | 4 | 4 | 4 | 4 | 4 | 4 | 72 |
| £11,875 | Round 3 | 3 | 4 | 4 | 4 | 3 | 4 | 5 | 5 | 3 | 4 | 5 | 3 | 4 | 4 | 4 | 4 | 4 | 4 | 71 |
| | Round 4 | 2 | 4 | 4 | 4 | 4 | 4 | 4 | 4 | 3 | 4 | 4 | 3 | 4 | 4 | 4 | 4 | 4 | 4 | 68-281 |
| ***Tiger Woods** | Round 1 | 3 | 3 | 4 | 4 | 3 | 5 | 4 | 5 | 3 | 6 | 6 | 3 | 4 | 4 | 4 | 4 | 5 | 5 | 75 |
| USA | Round 2 | 4 | 4 | 5 | 4 | 3 | 4 | 4 | 3 | 3 | 4 | 5 | 2 | 3 | 3 | 4 | 3 | 5 | 3 | 66 |
| | Round 3 | 2 | 4 | 4 | 4 | 3 | 4 | 4 | 4 | 3 | 5 | 5 | 4 | 4 | 4 | 4 | 4 | 4 | 4 | 70 |
| | Round 4 | 3 | 5 | 4 | 5 | 2 | 5 | 4 | 4 | 3 | 3 | 4 | 3 | 5 | 4 | 4 | 3 | 4 | 5 | 70-281 |
| **Carl Mason** | Round 1 | 2 | 3 | 4 | 3 | 4 | 4 | 4 | 4 | 3 | 3 | 5 | 3 | 4 | 4 | 5 | 3 | 5 | 5 | 68 |
| England | Round 2 | 3 | 3 | 4 | 4 | 3 | 4 | 5 | 4 | 2 | 4 | 4 | 3 | 3 | 4 | 4 | 4 | 7 | 5 | 70 |
| £11,875 | Round 3 | 4 | 3 | 4 | 4 | 2 | 5 | 4 | 3 | 3 | 3 | 5 | 3 | 4 | 4 | 3 | 5 | 7 | 4 | 70 |
| | Round 4 | 2 | 4 | 4 | 4 | 4 | 4 | 5 | 4 | 3 | 5 | 7 | 3 | 3 | 5 | 3 | 4 | 5 | 4 | 73-281 |
| **Steve Stricker** | Round 1 | 2 | 5 | 3 | 4 | 3 | 4 | 5 | 4 | 3 | 4 | 4 | 3 | 4 | 4 | 6 | 4 | 5 | 4 | 71 |
| USA | Round 2 | 3 | 5 | 4 | 3 | 3 | 4 | 3 | 4 | 4 | 3 | 4 | 4 | 4 | 4 | 4 | 5 | 5 | 4 | 70 |
| £11,875 | Round 3 | 2 | 4 | 4 | 4 | 3 | 4 | 4 | 3 | 3 | 4 | 5 | 3 | 4 | 4 | 4 | 4 | 4 | 3 | 66 |
| | Round 4 | 3 | 4 | 4 | 5 | 3 | 5 | 5 | 4 | 3 | 4 | 4 | 5 | 5 | 4 | 4 | 4 | 4 | 4 | 74-281 |
| **Ben Crenshaw** | Round 1 | 3 | 4 | 4 | 4 | 3 | 6 | 5 | 4 | 3 | 4 | 4 | 3 | 4 | 4 | 4 | 4 | 6 | 4 | 73 |
| USA | Round 2 | 3 | 3 | 5 | 3 | 4 | 4 | 4 | 4 | 3 | 5 | 4 | 3 | 4 | 4 | 3 | 3 | 5 | 4 | 68 |
| £9,525 | Round 3 | 4 | 4 | 4 | 4 | 3 | 5 | 5 | 4 | 3 | 4 | 4 | 3 | 3 | 4 | 4 | 4 | 4 | 5 | 71 |
| | Round 4 | 4 | 4 | 3 | 3 | 3 | 4 | 5 | 5 | 3 | 4 | 5 | 3 | 4 | 4 | 4 | 4 | 4 | 4 | 70-282 |
| **Tom Kite** | Round 1 | 3 | 5 | 5 | 4 | 3 | 5 | 4 | 4 | 3 | 5 | 5 | 4 | 3 | 6 | 5 | 4 | 5 | 4 | 77 |
| USA | Round 2 | 3 | 4 | 5 | 4 | 3 | 5 | 4 | 4 | 4 | 4 | 3 | 3 | 3 | 4 | 3 | 3 | 3 | 4 | 66 |
| £9,525 | Round 3 | 3 | 4 | 3 | 4 | 2 | 4 | 4 | 5 | 3 | 4 | 5 | 3 | 4 | 4 | 5 | 4 | 4 | 4 | 69 |
| | Round 4 | 3 | 7 | 4 | 4 | 4 | 4 | 3 | 4 | 2 | 5 | 5 | 2 | 4 | 4 | 4 | 3 | 4 | 4 | 70-282 |
| **Paul Broadhurst** | Round 1 | 3 | 4 | 4 | 4 | 3 | 3 | 5 | 4 | 2 | 3 | 4 | 3 | 4 | 4 | 4 | 4 | 3 | 4 | 65 |
| England | Round 2 | 3 | 4 | 3 | 5 | 3 | 5 | 4 | 5 | 4 | 6 | 3 | 3 | 4 | 5 | 4 | 3 | 4 | 4 | 72 |
| £9,525 | Round 3 | 2 | 4 | 4 | 4 | 3 | 5 | 5 | 4 | 3 | 4 | 6 | 5 | 4 | 4 | 5 | 4 | 4 | 4 | 74 |
| | Round 4 | 3 | 4 | 4 | 4 | 3 | 5 | 4 | 4 | 3 | 4 | 6 | 4 | 3 | 4 | 4 | 4 | 4 | 4 | 71-282 |
| **Corey Pavin** | Round 1 | 3 | 4 | 4 | 4 | 2 | 5 | 5 | 4 | 4 | 4 | 5 | 2 | 3 | 4 | 4 | 5 | 4 | 4 | 70 |
| USA | Round 2 | 2 | 4 | 5 | 4 | 3 | 4 | 5 | 4 | 2 | 4 | 4 | 3 | 3 | 4 | 3 | 4 | 4 | 4 | 66 |
| £9,525 | Round 3 | 3 | 4 | 5 | 3 | 3 | 5 | 5 | 5 | 3 | 5 | 5 | 3 | 5 | 4 | 4 | 4 | 4 | 4 | 74 |
| | Round 4 | 3 | 5 | 4 | 3 | 3 | 6 | 4 | 5 | 3 | 4 | 5 | 3 | 3 | 5 | 4 | 4 | 4 | 4 | 72-282 |
| **Peter Mitchell** | Round 1 | 3 | 4 | 5 | 3 | 3 | 5 | 4 | 4 | 3 | 3 | 5 | 5 | 4 | 4 | 4 | 3 | 4 | 5 | 71 |
| England | Round 2 | 2 | 4 | 4 | 4 | 3 | 4 | 4 | 4 | 3 | 5 | 5 | 3 | 4 | 4 | 3 | 3 | 4 | 5 | 68 |
| £9,525 | Round 3 | 3 | 5 | 4 | 4 | 3 | 4 | 4 | 4 | 2 | 5 | 5 | 3 | 5 | 4 | 4 | 4 | 4 | 4 | 71 |
| | Round 4 | 3 | 4 | 3 | 4 | 4 | 5 | 4 | 4 | 3 | 4 | 6 | 3 | 4 | 4 | 5 | 4 | 4 | 4 | 72-282 |
| **Frank Nobilo** | Round 1 | 3 | 4 | 4 | 4 | 3 | 4 | 5 | 4 | 3 | 4 | 4 | 3 | 4 | 4 | 4 | 4 | 5 | 4 | 70 |
| New Zealand | Round 2 | 2 | 4 | 6 | 4 | 4 | 4 | 4 | 4 | 3 | 4 | 5 | 3 | 4 | 4 | 4 | 4 | 5 | 4 | 72 |
| £9,525 | Round 3 | 5 | 4 | 4 | 3 | 3 | 4 | 5 | 4 | 2 | 4 | 5 | 3 | 3 | 3 | 4 | 4 | 4 | 4 | 68 |
| | Round 4 | 3 | 4 | 4 | 5 | 4 | 4 | 4 | 4 | 3 | 3 | 5 | 4 | 3 | 4 | 4 | 4 | 4 | 6 | 72-282 |

| HOLE | | 1 | 2 | 3 | 4 | 5 | 6 | 7 | 8 | 9 | 10 | 11 | 12 | 13 | 14 | 15 | 16 | 17 | 18 | |
|---|---|---|---|---|---|---|---|---|---|---|---|---|---|---|---|---|---|---|---|---|
| PAR | | 3 | 4 | 4 | 4 | 3 | 5 | 5 | 4 | 3 | 4 | 5 | 3 | 4 | 4 | 4 | 4 | 4 | 4 | TOTAL |
| **Edward Romero** | Round 1 | 3 | 4 | 5 | 4 | 3 | 3 | 4 | 4 | 4 | 4 | 5 | 3 | 5 | 3 | 4 | 4 | 4 | 4 | 70 |
| Argentina | Round 2 | 3 | 4 | 4 | 4 | 3 | 5 | 4 | 4 | 3 | 3 | 5 | 3 | 3 | 3 | 5 | 4 | 6 | 5 | 71 |
| £7,844 | Round 3 | 3 | 4 | 6 | 5 | 2 | 4 | 5 | 5 | 3 | 5 | 5 | 3 | 4 | 4 | 4 | 5 | 4 | 4 | 75 |
| | Round 4 | 2 | 4 | 4 | 5 | 3 | 4 | 4 | 4 | 2 | 4 | 4 | 3 | 4 | 4 | 4 | 4 | 4 | 4 | 67-283 |
| **Tommy Tolles** | Round 1 | 4 | 4 | 5 | 4 | 3 | 5 | 5 | 5 | 4 | 4 | 5 | 2 | 4 | 4 | 4 | 3 | 4 | 4 | 73 |
| USA | Round 2 | 3 | 6 | 4 | 5 | 3 | 4 | 4 | 3 | 3 | 3 | 5 | 3 | 4 | 4 | 4 | 4 | 4 | 4 | 70 |
| £7,844 | Round 3 | 3 | 3 | 4 | 6 | 2 | 5 | 4 | 4 | 4 | 3 | 4 | 3 | 6 | 4 | 4 | 3 | 4 | 5 | 71 |
| | Round 4 | 3 | 3 | 3 | 4 | 3 | 4 | 5 | 4 | 2 | 4 | 5 | 3 | 4 | 5 | 5 | 3 | 5 | 4 | 69-283 |
| **Scott Simpson** | Round 1 | 3 | 4 | 4 | 4 | 3 | 5 | 5 | 3 | 3 | 4 | 4 | 3 | 3 | 4 | 5 | 5 | 4 | 5 | 71 |
| USA | Round 2 | 3 | 4 | 4 | 3 | 4 | 4 | 5 | 4 | 2 | 3 | 5 | 3 | 4 | 4 | 5 | 4 | 4 | 4 | 69 |
| £7,844 | Round 3 | 2 | 4 | 6 | 4 | 3 | 5 | 3 | 4 | 3 | 4 | 5 | 3 | 4 | 5 | 4 | 6 | 4 | 4 | 73 |
| | Round 4 | 3 | 4 | 4 | 4 | 3 | 4 | 5 | 3 | 3 | 4 | 5 | 4 | 3 | 4 | 4 | 4 | 5 | 4 | 70-283 |
| **Eamonn Darcy** | Round 1 | 3 | 4 | 4 | 4 | 3 | 5 | 5 | 5 | 3 | 4 | 4 | 4 | 4 | 4 | 4 | 4 | 5 | 4 | 73 |
| Ireland | Round 2 | 3 | 4 | 4 | 4 | 3 | 4 | 6 | 4 | 2 | 3 | 5 | 4 | 3 | 5 | 4 | 3 | 4 | 4 | 69 |
| £7,844 | Round 3 | 2 | 3 | 5 | 4 | 3 | 5 | 5 | 5 | 3 | 3 | 5 | 3 | 4 | 4 | 4 | 4 | 5 | 4 | 71 |
| | Round 4 | 3 | 4 | 4 | 5 | 4 | 4 | 4 | 4 | 3 | 4 | 6 | 2 | 4 | 4 | 4 | 3 | 4 | 4 | 70-283 |
| **David Gilford** | Round 1 | 4 | 4 | 4 | 4 | 3 | 5 | 5 | 4 | 3 | 4 | 5 | 3 | 4 | 4 | 3 | 3 | 5 | 4 | 71 |
| England | Round 2 | 2 | 4 | 4 | 4 | 3 | 5 | 4 | 3 | 3 | 5 | 4 | 3 | 4 | 4 | 4 | 4 | 4 | 3 | 67 |
| £7,844 | Round 3 | 4 | 4 | 4 | 4 | 3 | 4 | 5 | 5 | 2 | 4 | 5 | 3 | 5 | 4 | 4 | 4 | 4 | 3 | 71 |
| | Round 4 | 3 | 4 | 4 | 4 | 4 | 4 | 3 | 5 | 3 | 4 | 5 | 3 | 4 | 6 | 5 | 4 | 5 | 4 | 74-283 |
| **Mark O'Meara** | Round 1 | 2 | 5 | 4 | 4 | 2 | 4 | 4 | 4 | 3 | 4 | 5 | 3 | 3 | 4 | 4 | 4 | 3 | 5 | 67 |
| USA | Round 2 | 3 | 4 | 3 | 4 | 3 | 4 | 4 | 3 | 3 | 4 | 5 | 3 | 5 | 4 | 4 | 4 | 4 | 5 | 69 |
| £7,844 | Round 3 | 2 | 4 | 4 | 4 | 4 | 5 | 5 | 4 | 3 | 4 | 4 | 5 | 4 | 4 | 3 | 4 | 4 | 5 | 72 |
| | Round 4 | 3 | 4 | 6 | 5 | 3 | 6 | 6 | 5 | 3 | 3 | 5 | 3 | 4 | 4 | 4 | 3 | 4 | 4 | 75-283 |
| **Hidemichi Tanaka** | Round 1 | 3 | 3 | 4 | 4 | 3 | 4 | 5 | 3 | 2 | 3 | 4 | 3 | 4 | 4 | 4 | 4 | 4 | 4 | 67 |
| Japan | Round 2 | 3 | 5 | 4 | 5 | 3 | 5 | 5 | 4 | 3 | 3 | 4 | 4 | 5 | 4 | 3 | 4 | 4 | 3 | 71 |
| £7,844 | Round 3 | 4 | 4 | 4 | 5 | 3 | 4 | 4 | 5 | 2 | 4 | 3 | 2 | 4 | 4 | 4 | 4 | 5 | 5 | 70 |
| | Round 4 | 3 | 5 | 4 | 4 | 3 | 4 | 4 | 4 | 3 | 5 | 5 | 4 | 5 | 4 | 4 | 4 | 6 | 4 | 75-283 |
| **Brad Faxon** | Round 1 | 3 | 4 | 4 | 4 | 2 | 4 | 5 | 4 | 2 | 4 | 5 | 3 | 3 | 4 | 4 | 4 | 4 | 4 | 67 |
| USA | Round 2 | 4 | 4 | 5 | 5 | 3 | 6 | 5 | 5 | 3 | 4 | 4 | 3 | 4 | 3 | 4 | 3 | 4 | 4 | 73 |
| £7,844 | Round 3 | 3 | 4 | 4 | 3 | 4 | 4 | 4 | 4 | 2 | 4 | 5 | 3 | 3 | 5 | 4 | 4 | 4 | 4 | 68 |
| | Round 4 | 3 | 4 | 5 | 5 | 3 | 5 | 5 | 4 | 2 | 4 | 5 | 3 | 4 | 4 | 5 | 4 | 6 | 4 | 75-283 |
| **Mark Calcavecchia** | Round 1 | 3 | 4 | 4 | 4 | 3 | 5 | 5 | 4 | 3 | 4 | 5 | 2 | 4 | 4 | 4 | 4 | 4 | 6 | 72 |
| USA | Round 2 | 3 | 4 | 4 | 4 | 3 | 4 | 4 | 4 | 2 | 4 | 4 | 3 | 4 | 4 | 4 | 4 | 5 | 4 | 68 |
| £7,150 | Round 3 | 3 | 4 | 5 | 4 | 2 | 5 | 8 | 4 | 3 | 4 | 5 | 3 | 4 | 7 | 4 | 3 | 4 | 4 | 76 |
| | Round 4 | 3 | 3 | 4 | 4 | 4 | 5 | 6 | 4 | 3 | 3 | 4 | 3 | 4 | 3 | 3 | 3 | 4 | 5 | 68-284 |
| **Phil Mickelson** | Round 1 | 3 | 3 | 3 | 4 | 3 | 5 | 5 | 4 | 3 | 4 | 6 | 4 | 4 | 4 | 5 | 3 | 4 | 5 | 72 |
| USA | Round 2 | 3 | 4 | 4 | 5 | 4 | 5 | 5 | 4 | 2 | 3 | 5 | 4 | 3 | 4 | 4 | 4 | 4 | 4 | 71 |
| £7,150 | Round 3 | 3 | 4 | 4 | 4 | 3 | 4 | 5 | 5 | 3 | 4 | 5 | 3 | 3 | 4 | 4 | 4 | 5 | 5 | 72 |
| | Round 4 | 3 | 5 | 4 | 4 | 3 | 4 | 4 | 4 | 3 | 3 | 5 | 3 | 4 | 3 | 5 | 4 | 4 | 4 | 69-284 |
| **Klas Eriksson** | Round 1 | 4 | 4 | 3 | 5 | 3 | 4 | 4 | 3 | 2 | 4 | 5 | 4 | 4 | 4 | 4 | 3 | 4 | 4 | 68 |
| Sweden | Round 2 | 3 | 3 | 5 | 4 | 4 | 5 | 6 | 4 | 2 | 4 | 6 | 2 | 4 | 5 | 5 | 4 | 4 | 5 | 75 |
| £7,150 | Round 3 | 4 | 3 | 4 | 5 | 3 | 4 | 6 | 3 | 3 | 4 | 6 | 3 | 4 | 4 | 4 | 4 | 4 | 4 | 72 |
| | Round 4 | 3 | 4 | 3 | 4 | 3 | 4 | 5 | 6 | 4 | 3 | 5 | 3 | 3 | 3 | 4 | 5 | 3 | 4 | 69-284 |
| **David Frost** | Round 1 | 3 | 5 | 4 | 4 | 3 | 5 | 4 | 3 | 3 | 4 | 5 | 3 | 4 | 4 | 4 | 4 | 4 | 4 | 70 |
| South Africa | Round 2 | 3 | 4 | 4 | 5 | 3 | 7 | 4 | 4 | 3 | 5 | 6 | 3 | 3 | 4 | 3 | 3 | 4 | 4 | 72 |
| £7,150 | Round 3 | 3 | 5 | 4 | 4 | 3 | 4 | 4 | 3 | 3 | 4 | 5 | 3 | 5 | 4 | 4 | 4 | 4 | 5 | 71 |
| | Round 4 | 3 | 4 | 4 | 4 | 4 | 4 | 4 | 5 | 5 | 3 | 4 | 4 | 3 | 4 | 4 | 4 | 4 | 4 | 71-284 |

| | | 1 | 2 | 3 | 4 | 5 | 6 | 7 | 8 | 9 | 10 | 11 | 12 | 13 | 14 | 15 | 16 | 17 | 18 | |
|---|---|---|---|---|---|---|---|---|---|---|---|---|---|---|---|---|---|---|---|---|
| HOLE | | | | | | | | | | | | | | | | | | | | |
| PAR | | 3 | 4 | 4 | 4 | 3 | 5 | 5 | 4 | 3 | 4 | 5 | 3 | 4 | 4 | 4 | 4 | 4 | 4 | TOTAL |
| Craig Stadler | Round 1 | 3 | 3 | 5 | 4 | 3 | 4 | 4 | 3 | 3 | 4 | 6 | 3 | 5 | 4 | 4 | 4 | 5 | 4 | 71 |
| USA | Round 2 | 3 | 4 | 6 | 4 | 4 | 4 | 4 | 4 | 4 | 4 | 3 | 3 | 3 | 4 | 4 | 4 | 4 | 5 | 71 |
| £6,400 | Round 3 | 3 | 3 | 4 | 4 | 3 | 5 | 4 | 5 | 3 | 4 | 7 | 3 | 5 | 5 | 4 | 4 | 4 | 5 | 75 |
| | Round 4 | 3 | 4 | 4 | 4 | 3 | 5 | 5 | 4 | 2 | 4 | 5 | 3 | 4 | 4 | 3 | 3 | 4 | 4 | 68-285 |
| Billy Mayfair | Round 1 | 3 | 4 | 5 | 4 | 3 | 4 | 4 | 4 | 3 | 4 | 4 | 3 | 4 | 4 | 4 | 4 | 5 | 4 | 70 |
| USA | Round 2 | 3 | 5 | 5 | 4 | 3 | 4 | 5 | 3 | 3 | 5 | 4 | 3 | 4 | 4 | 5 | 4 | 3 | 5 | 72 |
| £6,400 | Round 3 | 3 | 4 | 4 | 4 | 3 | 3 | 7 | 4 | 3 | 4 | 5 | 4 | 5 | 4 | 4 | 4 | 5 | 4 | 74 |
| | Round 4 | 3 | 4 | 3 | 4 | 3 | 4 | 5 | 4 | 2 | 4 | 5 | 3 | 5 | 4 | 4 | 4 | 4 | 4 | 69-285 |
| Peter Jacobsen | Round 1 | 3 | 4 | 5 | 4 | 3 | 5 | 4 | 4 | 3 | 3 | 5 | 4 | 4 | 4 | 4 | 4 | 4 | 5 | 72 |
| USA | Round 2 | 3 | 4 | 4 | 4 | 3 | 4 | 5 | 5 | 2 | 5 | 5 | 3 | 4 | 4 | 4 | 3 | 4 | 4 | 70 |
| £6,400 | Round 3 | 3 | 5 | 4 | 5 | 3 | 5 | 5 | 4 | 3 | 5 | 4 | 3 | 4 | 5 | 4 | 4 | 4 | 4 | 74 |
| | Round 4 | 3 | 4 | 4 | 3 | 3 | 5 | 4 | 3 | 2 | 4 | 5 | 4 | 4 | 4 | 4 | 4 | 5 | 4 | 69-285 |
| Todd Hamilton | Round 1 | 3 | 4 | 4 | 4 | 3 | 4 | 4 | 4 | 3 | 5 | 5 | 3 | 4 | 4 | 4 | 5 | 5 | 4 | 71 |
| USA | Round 2 | 3 | 6 | 4 | 3 | 3 | 4 | 4 | 4 | 3 | 4 | 4 | 3 | 4 | 4 | 4 | 4 | 4 | 5 | 70 |
| £6,400 | Round 3 | 2 | 5 | 5 | 4 | 2 | 5 | 5 | 5 | 3 | 5 | 6 | 4 | 3 | 3 | 5 | 4 | 5 | 3 | 74 |
| | Round 4 | 3 | 4 | 5 | 4 | 2 | 4 | 4 | 4 | 2 | 4 | 4 | 4 | 4 | 4 | 4 | 4 | 6 | 4 | 70-285 |
| Bradley Hughes | Round 1 | 3 | 5 | 4 | 3 | 4 | 5 | 4 | 4 | 3 | 3 | 4 | 3 | 4 | 5 | 4 | 4 | 4 | 4 | 70 |
| Australia | Round 2 | 4 | 4 | 4 | 4 | 3 | 4 | 4 | 4 | 3 | 4 | 4 | 2 | 4 | 4 | 5 | 4 | 5 | 4 | 69 |
| £6,400 | Round 3 | 3 | 4 | 4 | 5 | 3 | 4 | 5 | 4 | 3 | 3 | 5 | 5 | 4 | 4 | 6 | 3 | 4 | 6 | 75 |
| | Round 4 | 3 | 4 | 4 | 4 | 3 | 3 | 5 | 5 | 2 | 4 | 6 | 3 | 4 | 4 | 4 | 4 | 4 | 5 | 71-285 |
| Payne Stewart | Round 1 | 3 | 4 | 5 | 3 | 3 | 5 | 5 | 4 | 3 | 4 | 5 | 2 | 3 | 4 | 4 | 4 | 5 | 4 | 70 |
| USA | Round 2 | 3 | 4 | 5 | 3 | 4 | 6 | 4 | 5 | 3 | 5 | 5 | 3 | 4 | 4 | 4 | 4 | 3 | 4 | 73 |
| £6,400 | Round 3 | 3 | 4 | 4 | 4 | 3 | 3 | 5 | 4 | 3 | 4 | 6 | 3 | 4 | 4 | 4 | 4 | 5 | 4 | 71 |
| | Round 4 | 3 | 4 | 4 | 3 | 3 | 4 | 4 | 4 | 3 | 4 | 6 | 4 | 3 | 5 | 5 | 4 | 4 | 4 | 71-285 |
| Richard Boxall | Round 1 | 3 | 4 | 5 | 4 | 3 | 3 | 4 | 4 | 3 | 4 | 5 | 4 | 5 | 4 | 5 | 4 | 4 | 4 | 72 |
| England | Round 2 | 2 | 4 | 4 | 5 | 3 | 4 | 5 | 4 | 2 | 5 | 6 | 3 | 4 | 5 | 4 | 4 | 3 | 3 | 70 |
| £6,400 | Round 3 | 4 | 3 | 4 | 4 | 3 | 4 | 6 | 4 | 3 | 4 | 6 | 3 | 4 | 4 | 3 | 4 | 4 | 4 | 71 |
| | Round 4 | 3 | 4 | 3 | 4 | 3 | 5 | 5 | 4 | 2 | 4 | 6 | 4 | 4 | 4 | 5 | 4 | 4 | 4 | 72-285 |
| Jack Nicklaus | Round 1 | 3 | 4 | 4 | 5 | 3 | 3 | 5 | 4 | 3 | 4 | 4 | 2 | 3 | 4 | 5 | 5 | 4 | 4 | 69 |
| USA | Round 2 | 2 | 4 | 4 | 4 | 3 | 5 | 4 | 4 | 2 | 3 | 5 | 3 | 4 | 3 | 4 | 4 | 4 | 4 | 66 |
| £6,400 | Round 3 | 4 | 4 | 5 | 4 | 3 | 4 | 6 | 4 | 3 | 5 | 5 | 4 | 4 | 5 | 4 | 5 | 5 | 3 | 77 |
| | Round 4 | 3 | 3 | 4 | 4 | 4 | 4 | 5 | 4 | 3 | 4 | 5 | 3 | 5 | 4 | 6 | 4 | 4 | 4 | 73-285 |
| Nick Price | Round 1 | 3 | 4 | 4 | 5 | 3 | 3 | 4 | 4 | 2 | 4 | 5 | 3 | 3 | 3 | 5 | 4 | 5 | 4 | 68 |
| Zimbabwe | Round 2 | 3 | 4 | 4 | 4 | 3 | 5 | 4 | 5 | 3 | 4 | 5 | 3 | 5 | 5 | 3 | 4 | 5 | 4 | 73 |
| £6,400 | Round 3 | 3 | 3 | 4 | 4 | 3 | 4 | 5 | 4 | 3 | 4 | 5 | 4 | 4 | 5 | 4 | 4 | 4 | 4 | 71 |
| | Round 4 | 3 | 5 | 4 | 4 | 3 | 5 | 4 | 5 | 3 | 4 | 5 | 4 | 3 | 3 | 5 | 6 | 3 | 4 | 73-285 |
| Jim Furyk | Round 1 | 3 | 4 | 4 | 4 | 3 | 4 | 5 | 4 | 3 | 3 | 4 | 4 | 5 | 3 | 4 | 4 | 4 | 3 | 68 |
| USA | Round 2 | 3 | 4 | 4 | 4 | 3 | 5 | 5 | 4 | 3 | 4 | 5 | 3 | 4 | 3 | 4 | 4 | 5 | 4 | 71 |
| £6,400 | Round 3 | 3 | 4 | 3 | 3 | 3 | 4 | 5 | 5 | 5 | 4 | 5 | 3 | 4 | 4 | 5 | 4 | 3 | 5 | 72 |
| | Round 4 | 3 | 6 | 4 | 4 | 4 | 5 | 3 | 4 | 2 | 4 | 5 | 2 | 4 | 6 | 4 | 4 | 5 | 5 | 74-285 |
| Jesper Parnevik | Round 1 | 3 | 4 | 4 | 3 | 3 | 5 | 5 | 5 | 3 | 5 | 4 | 4 | 4 | 4 | 4 | 4 | 4 | 4 | 72 |
| Sweden | Round 2 | 4 | 4 | 4 | 4 | 3 | 5 | 4 | 4 | 3 | 3 | 4 | 3 | 4 | 4 | 5 | 3 | 4 | 4 | 69 |
| £6,400 | Round 3 | 3 | 3 | 4 | 4 | 3 | 4 | 5 | 4 | 3 | 4 | 6 | 4 | 3 | 4 | 4 | 3 | 4 | 4 | 69 |
| | Round 4 | 3 | 5 | 5 | 5 | 4 | 4 | 5 | 4 | 3 | 3 | 5 | 3 | 4 | 4 | 5 | 5 | 4 | 4 | 75-285 |
| Jim Payne | Round 1 | 2 | 4 | 4 | 5 | 3 | 5 | 4 | 4 | 3 | 5 | 6 | 2 | 4 | 4 | 4 | 4 | 5 | 4 | 72 |
| England | Round 2 | 3 | 4 | 4 | 5 | 3 | 4 | 4 | 4 | 3 | 4 | 4 | 3 | 4 | 4 | 6 | 4 | 3 | 5 | 71 |
| £5,688 | Round 3 | 3 | 4 | 4 | 3 | 3 | 5 | 4 | 5 | 3 | 3 | 5 | 4 | 4 | 5 | 5 | 5 | 4 | 4 | 73 |
| | Round 4 | 3 | 5 | 4 | 3 | 3 | 5 | 5 | 4 | 2 | 3 | 3 | 3 | 4 | 5 | 5 | 4 | 4 | 5 | 70-286 |

| | | 1 | 2 | 3 | 4 | 5 | 6 | 7 | 8 | 9 | 10 | 11 | 12 | 13 | 14 | 15 | 16 | 17 | 18 | TOTAL |
|---|---|---|---|---|---|---|---|---|---|---|---|---|---|---|---|---|---|---|---|---|
| HOLE | | 1 | 2 | 3 | 4 | 5 | 6 | 7 | 8 | 9 | 10 | 11 | 12 | 13 | 14 | 15 | 16 | 17 | 18 | |
| PAR | | 3 | 4 | 4 | 4 | 3 | 5 | 5 | 4 | 3 | 4 | 5 | 3 | 4 | 4 | 4 | 4 | 4 | 4 | TOTAL |
| **Sandy Lyle** | Round 1 | 3 | 4 | 4 | 4 | 3 | 4 | 4 | 4 | 3 | 4 | 4 | 3 | 5 | 4 | 5 | 4 | 5 | 4 | 71 |
| Scotland | Round 2 | 2 | 4 | 4 | 4 | 3 | 4 | 4 | 4 | 3 | 4 | 5 | 3 | 5 | 5 | 3 | 4 | 4 | 4 | 69 |
| £5,688 | Round 3 | 3 | 4 | 4 | 4 | 3 | 6 | 5 | 4 | 3 | 4 | 5 | 4 | 4 | 4 | 5 | 3 | 4 | 4 | 73 |
| | Round 4 | 3 | 4 | 3 | 5 | 3 | 5 | 5 | 5 | 3 | 4 | 6 | 3 | 3 | 4 | 4 | 4 | 5 | 4 | 73-286 |
| **Robert Allenby** | Round 1 | 2 | 5 | 7 | 4 | 3 | 3 | 5 | 5 | 3 | 4 | 5 | 4 | 4 | 3 | 5 | 4 | 4 | 4 | 74 |
| Australia | Round 2 | 3 | 3 | 5 | 5 | 3 | 5 | 4 | 3 | 3 | 3 | 4 | 3 | 4 | 4 | 4 | 4 | 4 | 4 | 68 |
| £5,688 | Round 3 | 2 | 4 | 4 | 5 | 3 | 4 | 4 | 4 | 3 | 5 | 5 | 3 | 4 | 5 | 5 | 3 | 3 | 5 | 71 |
| | Round 4 | 3 | 4 | 4 | 4 | 3 | 5 | 6 | 5 | 2 | 4 | 5 | 4 | 4 | 4 | 4 | 4 | 4 | 4 | 73-286 |
| **Stephen Ames** | Round 1 | 3 | 4 | 4 | 4 | 3 | 4 | 4 | 3 | 3 | 5 | 5 | 3 | 4 | 4 | 4 | 4 | 6 | 4 | 71 |
| Trinidad & Tobago | Round 2 | 2 | 4 | 3 | 4 | 4 | 5 | 5 | 4 | 3 | 4 | 5 | 3 | 4 | 4 | 4 | 6 | 4 | 4 | 72 |
| £5,688 | Round 3 | 3 | 4 | 5 | 4 | 3 | 4 | 5 | 4 | 2 | 4 | 5 | 3 | 3 | 4 | 4 | 4 | 4 | 4 | 69 |
| | Round 4 | 3 | 4 | 4 | 4 | 3 | 5 | 4 | 5 | 2 | 4 | 6 | 2 | 4 | 4 | 5 | 4 | 6 | 5 | 74-286 |
| **Michael Jonzon** | Round 1 | 3 | 4 | 4 | 5 | 2 | 4 | 5 | 3 | 3 | 3 | 6 | 3 | 4 | 4 | 4 | 4 | 5 | 3 | 69 |
| Sweden | Round 2 | 3 | 4 | 4 | 4 | 5 | 6 | 5 | 4 | 2 | 3 | 5 | 3 | 4 | 5 | 4 | 4 | 4 | 4 | 73 |
| £5,475 | Round 3 | 4 | 4 | 3 | 5 | 2 | 4 | 6 | 4 | 4 | 4 | 5 | 3 | 4 | 5 | 4 | 4 | 4 | 4 | 73 |
| | Round 4 | 3 | 4 | 6 | 3 | 4 | 5 | 3 | 4 | 2 | 4 | 5 | 3 | 4 | 4 | 4 | 5 | 4 | 5 | 72-287 |
| **D. A. Weibring** | Round 1 | 3 | 5 | 4 | 4 | 3 | 5 | 4 | 4 | 3 | 3 | 5 | 3 | 4 | 4 | 5 | 3 | 3 | 6 | 71 |
| USA | Round 2 | 2 | 4 | 4 | 4 | 4 | 3 | 4 | 5 | 3 | 4 | 5 | 4 | 4 | 4 | 5 | 4 | 4 | 5 | 72 |
| £5,475 | Round 3 | 4 | 3 | 5 | 4 | 3 | 4 | 4 | 4 | 3 | 6 | 5 | 4 | 3 | 5 | 3 | 4 | 4 | 4 | 72 |
| | Round 4 | 3 | 4 | 3 | 4 | 4 | 4 | 5 | 4 | 3 | 5 | 5 | 3 | 4 | 4 | 4 | 4 | 5 | 4 | 72-287 |
| **Jeff Sluman** | Round 1 | 3 | 4 | 5 | 4 | 3 | 5 | 3 | 4 | 3 | 4 | 5 | 3 | 3 | 5 | 5 | 4 | 5 | 4 | 72 |
| USA | Round 2 | 3 | 4 | 4 | 5 | 2 | 5 | 4 | 4 | 3 | 4 | 5 | 4 | 4 | 4 | 4 | 4 | 4 | 3 | 70 |
| £5,475 | Round 3 | 3 | 4 | 4 | 5 | 3 | 4 | 4 | 5 | 3 | 5 | 4 | 3 | 4 | 4 | 4 | 4 | 4 | 3 | 70 |
| | Round 4 | 3 | 4 | 5 | 4 | 3 | 4 | 4 | 4 | 3 | 4 | 5 | 4 | 5 | 4 | 5 | 4 | 6 | 4 | 75-287 |
| **Brian Barnes** | Round 1 | 3 | 4 | 4 | 4 | 4 | 5 | 5 | 4 | 4 | 3 | 4 | 4 | 4 | 4 | 5 | 4 | 4 | 4 | 73 |
| Scotland | Round 2 | 2 | 4 | 5 | 4 | 4 | 4 | 4 | 5 | 3 | 4 | 5 | 3 | 4 | 3 | 4 | 4 | 5 | 3 | 70 |
| £5,475 | Round 3 | 2 | 4 | 4 | 4 | 2 | 6 | 4 | 3 | 5 | 4 | 3 | 4 | 4 | 4 | 4 | 4 | 4 | 4 | 69 |
| | Round 4 | 3 | 4 | 6 | 4 | 3 | 6 | 4 | 5 | 3 | 4 | 5 | 4 | 4 | 4 | 4 | 4 | 4 | 4 | 75-287 |
| **Carl Suneson** | Round 1 | 3 | 5 | 6 | 4 | 3 | 4 | 5 | 4 | 3 | 4 | 5 | 3 | 4 | 4 | 4 | 4 | 4 | 4 | 73 |
| Spain | Round 2 | 2 | 4 | 4 | 4 | 4 | 4 | 3 | 5 | 3 | 4 | 5 | 3 | 4 | 4 | 4 | 4 | 4 | 4 | 69 |
| £5,300 | Round 3 | 2 | 4 | 5 | 4 | 3 | 5 | 5 | 5 | 3 | 4 | 5 | 3 | 3 | 5 | 4 | 5 | 5 | 4 | 74 |
| | Round 4 | 3 | 5 | 5 | 5 | 3 | 4 | 3 | 5 | 3 | 5 | 5 | 3 | 4 | 4 | 4 | 4 | 4 | 3 | 72-288 |
| **Costantino Rocca** | Round 1 | 2 | 5 | 4 | 4 | 3 | 5 | 4 | 4 | 4 | 4 | 4 | 3 | 5 | 4 | 4 | 4 | 4 | 4 | 71 |
| Italy | Round 2 | 3 | 4 | 4 | 4 | 4 | 4 | 4 | 4 | 2 | 3 | 4 | 3 | 4 | 5 | 4 | 5 | 5 | 4 | 70 |
| £5,300 | Round 3 | 4 | 5 | 5 | 4 | 2 | 3 | 5 | 4 | 3 | 5 | 5 | 3 | 4 | 5 | 4 | 5 | 4 | 4 | 74 |
| | Round 4 | 3 | 5 | 5 | 4 | 3 | 5 | 5 | 4 | 3 | 4 | 5 | 4 | 3 | 4 | 4 | 4 | 4 | 4 | 73-288 |
| **Gordon Law** | Round 1 | 3 | 4 | 4 | 5 | 3 | 5 | 4 | 4 | 3 | 4 | 6 | 3 | 4 | 4 | 5 | 4 | 5 | 4 | 74 |
| Scotland | Round 2 | 3 | 4 | 5 | 4 | 2 | 4 | 4 | 4 | 3 | 4 | 6 | 3 | 4 | 4 | 3 | 4 | 4 | 4 | 69 |
| £5,300 | Round 3 | 4 | 5 | 3 | 5 | 2 | 5 | 4 | 3 | 2 | 3 | 5 | 3 | 3 | 5 | 4 | 3 | 7 | 5 | 71 |
| | Round 4 | 3 | 5 | 4 | 4 | 3 | 4 | 5 | 4 | 4 | 4 | 4 | 4 | 4 | 4 | 5 | 5 | 4 | 4 | 74-288 |
| **David A. Russell** | Round 1 | 4 | 5 | 5 | 4 | 3 | 3 | 4 | 4 | 3 | 4 | 4 | 4 | 4 | 4 | 4 | 3 | 4 | 4 | 70 |
| England | Round 2 | 2 | 5 | 4 | 4 | 3 | 5 | 6 | 5 | 2 | 4 | 5 | 3 | 4 | 4 | 3 | 4 | 5 | 4 | 72 |
| £5,150 | Round 3 | 3 | 4 | 5 | 4 | 3 | 4 | 6 | 5 | 3 | 4 | 4 | 3 | 4 | 4 | 4 | 4 | 5 | 5 | 74 |
| | Round 4 | 3 | 5 | 5 | 4 | 4 | 5 | 4 | 5 | 4 | 3 | 5 | 4 | 4 | 4 | 3 | 4 | 3 | 4 | 73-289 |
| **Brett Ogle** | Round 1 | 3 | 3 | 4 | 4 | 5 | 5 | 3 | 4 | 3 | 4 | 5 | 3 | 3 | 4 | 4 | 5 | 4 | 4 | 70 |
| Australia | Round 2 | 3 | 4 | 7 | 4 | 2 | 5 | 8 | 4 | 3 | 4 | 4 | 3 | 4 | 4 | 3 | 4 | 4 | 3 | 73 |
| £5,150 | Round 3 | 3 | 4 | 4 | 4 | 4 | 4 | 5 | 4 | 3 | 4 | 5 | 3 | 4 | 4 | 5 | 6 | 3 | 4 | 73 |
| | Round 4 | 3 | 4 | 4 | 4 | 3 | 5 | 4 | 5 | 3 | 4 | 5 | 3 | 4 | 4 | 4 | 4 | 6 | 4 | 73-289 |

| HOLE | | 1 | 2 | 3 | 4 | 5 | 6 | 7 | 8 | 9 | 10 | 11 | 12 | 13 | 14 | 15 | 16 | 17 | 18 | |
|---|---|---|---|---|---|---|---|---|---|---|---|---|---|---|---|---|---|---|---|---|
| PAR | | 3 | 4 | 4 | 4 | 3 | 5 | 5 | 4 | 3 | 4 | 5 | 3 | 4 | 4 | 4 | 4 | 4 | 4 | TOTAL |
| **John Daly** | Round 1 | 3 | 4 | 3 | 4 | 2 | 4 | 4 | 4 | 3 | 4 | 4 | 4 | 5 | 4 | 4 | 5 | 5 | 4 | 70 |
| USA | Round 2 | 4 | 4 | 4 | 4 | 4 | 4 | 5 | 5 | 4 | 3 | 4 | 3 | 4 | 4 | 6 | 4 | 4 | 3 | 73 |
| £5,150 | Round 3 | 3 | 4 | 5 | 3 | 3 | 4 | 4 | 4 | 3 | 4 | 5 | 3 | 4 | 4 | 4 | 4 | 4 | 4 | 69 |
| | Round 4 | 4 | 5 | 5 | 6 | 3 | 4 | 6 | 4 | 3 | 4 | 4 | 3 | 3 | 5 | 4 | 4 | 4 | 6 | 77-289 |
| **Howard Clark** | Round 1 | 4 | 4 | 5 | 4 | 3 | 4 | 4 | 4 | 3 | 4 | 4 | 3 | 6 | 3 | 4 | 4 | 4 | 5 | 72 |
| England | Round 2 | 3 | 4 | 4 | 4 | 4 | 4 | 4 | 3 | 4 | 4 | 5 | 4 | 4 | 4 | 4 | 3 | 5 | 4 | 71 |
| £5,050 | Round 3 | 3 | 4 | 4 | 4 | 4 | 5 | 5 | 5 | 3 | 4 | 5 | 3 | 4 | 4 | 4 | 6 | 5 | 4 | 76 |
| | Round 4 | 3 | 4 | 5 | 5 | 3 | 4 | 4 | 5 | 2 | 6 | 5 | 3 | 3 | 4 | 3 | 4 | 4 | 4 | 71-290 |
| **Bob Charles** | Round 1 | 3 | 4 | 4 | 4 | 3 | 4 | 5 | 5 | 3 | 4 | 4 | 3 | 3 | 4 | 5 | 5 | 4 | 4 | 71 |
| New Zealand | Round 2 | 2 | 5 | 4 | 4 | 3 | 5 | 4 | 4 | 3 | 4 | 5 | 3 | 4 | 4 | 4 | 5 | 5 | 4 | 72 |
| £5,000 | Round 3 | 3 | 4 | 5 | 3 | 3 | 4 | 5 | 4 | 3 | 4 | 5 | 2 | 5 | 3 | 4 | 4 | 5 | 5 | 71 |
| | Round 4 | 3 | 4 | 8 | 5 | 3 | 5 | 4 | 4 | 3 | 5 | 4 | 3 | 4 | 4 | 5 | 4 | 5 | 4 | 77-291 |
| **Domingo Hospital** | Round 1 | 3 | 4 | 4 | 5 | 3 | 4 | 5 | 4 | 3 | 4 | 5 | 3 | 4 | 4 | 5 | 4 | 5 | 6 | 75 |
| Spain | Round 2 | 3 | 3 | 4 | 5 | 4 | 4 | 4 | 4 | 3 | 3 | 4 | 3 | 5 | 4 | 4 | 4 | 3 | 4 | 68 |
| £4,875 | Round 3 | 2 | 5 | 5 | 5 | 3 | 4 | 5 | 4 | 4 | 4 | 6 | 4 | 4 | 4 | 4 | 4 | 6 | 4 | 77 |
| | Round 4 | 3 | 4 | 4 | 4 | 3 | 4 | 4 | 4 | 3 | 4 | 6 | 3 | 4 | 4 | 5 | 3 | 5 | 5 | 72-292 |
| **Rick Todd** | Round 1 | 4 | 4 | 5 | 4 | 3 | 5 | 5 | 4 | 3 | 5 | 5 | 3 | 4 | 4 | 4 | 4 | 4 | 4 | 74 |
| Canada | Round 2 | 3 | 4 | 4 | 3 | 4 | 5 | 5 | 4 | 2 | 4 | 4 | 3 | 4 | 4 | 4 | 3 | 5 | 4 | 69 |
| £4,875 | Round 3 | 3 | 5 | 4 | 5 | 3 | 4 | 4 | 4 | 2 | 4 | 5 | 4 | 4 | 5 | 4 | 4 | 4 | 5 | 73 |
| | Round 4 | 4 | 4 | 4 | 4 | 3 | 6 | 4 | 5 | 3 | 4 | 4 | 3 | 5 | 5 | 4 | 3 | 7 | 4 | 76-292 |
| **Curtis Strange** | Round 1 | 4 | 4 | 4 | 5 | 3 | 4 | 4 | 4 | 3 | 5 | 5 | 3 | 4 | 4 | 4 | 4 | 3 | 4 | 71 |
| USA | Round 2 | 3 | 4 | 5 | 4 | 4 | 5 | 5 | 4 | 2 | 4 | 5 | 3 | 4 | 4 | 3 | 3 | 5 | 4 | 72 |
| £4,875 | Round 3 | 2 | 5 | 5 | 3 | 3 | 4 | 5 | 5 | 3 | 4 | 5 | 3 | 4 | 5 | 4 | 4 | 4 | 4 | 72 |
| | Round 4 | 5 | 4 | 3 | 5 | 3 | 7 | 5 | 4 | 3 | 5 | 6 | 3 | 3 | 4 | 5 | 4 | 4 | 4 | 77-292 |
| **Roger Chapman** | Round 1 | 3 | 4 | 4 | 3 | 3 | 3 | 5 | 7 | 3 | 4 | 5 | 3 | 4 | 4 | 4 | 4 | 5 | 4 | 72 |
| England | Round 2 | 3 | 4 | 4 | 5 | 3 | 4 | 4 | 4 | 3 | 3 | 4 | 3 | 4 | 4 | 5 | 5 | 3 | 5 | 70 |
| £4,875 | Round 3 | 3 | 4 | 4 | 4 | 3 | 5 | 4 | 4 | 3 | 4 | 5 | 2 | 3 | 4 | 4 | 4 | 5 | 5 | 70 |
| | Round 4 | 4 | 4 | 4 | 4 | 4 | 5 | 6 | 6 | 4 | 5 | 5 | 3 | 3 | 5 | 4 | 4 | 5 | 5 | 80-292 |
| **Retief Goosen** | Round 1 | 2 | 5 | 4 | 4 | 3 | 5 | 5 | 4 | 3 | 4 | 4 | 3 | 3 | 6 | 5 | 4 | 4 | 4 | 72 |
| South Africa | Round 2 | 5 | 4 | 5 | 4 | 4 | 4 | 4 | 5 | 3 | 3 | 4 | 2 | 3 | 4 | 4 | 5 | 5 | 3 | 71 |
| £4,750 | Round 3 | 3 | 5 | 5 | 4 | 3 | 4 | 4 | 4 | 3 | 4 | 4 | 4 | 4 | 4 | 5 | 4 | 5 | 5 | 74 |
| | Round 4 | 3 | 4 | 4 | 4 | 4 | 5 | 5 | 5 | 4 | 4 | 5 | 3 | 4 | 6 | 4 | 4 | 4 | 4 | 76-293 |
| **Arnaud Langenaeken** | Round 1 | 3 | 4 | 4 | 4 | 4 | 4 | 5 | 4 | 3 | 3 | 5 | 2 | 4 | 4 | 5 | 5 | 5 | 4 | 72 |
| Belgium | Round 2 | 2 | 5 | 5 | 3 | 2 | 4 | 5 | 5 | 3 | 4 | 4 | 4 | 6 | 3 | 4 | 4 | 4 | 4 | 71 |
| £4,700 | Round 3 | 4 | 4 | 4 | 4 | 4 | 4 | 5 | 6 | 4 | 4 | 5 | 3 | 4 | 4 | 4 | 4 | 5 | 5 | 77 |
| | Round 4 | 3 | 5 | 5 | 4 | 3 | 4 | 5 | 4 | 3 | 4 | 6 | 4 | 4 | 5 | 5 | 4 | 5 | 5 | 78-298 |

| HOLE | | 1 | 2 | 3 | 4 | 5 | 6 | 7 | 8 | 9 | 10 | 11 | 12 | 13 | 14 | 15 | 16 | 17 | 18 | |
|---|---|---|---|---|---|---|---|---|---|---|---|---|---|---|---|---|---|---|---|---|
| PAR | | 3 | 4 | 4 | 4 | 3 | 5 | 5 | 4 | 3 | 4 | 5 | 3 | 4 | 4 | 4 | 4 | 4 | 4 | TOTAL |

## NON QUALIFIERS AFTER 36 HOLES
*(All professionals receive £650)*

| Player | Round | 1 | 2 | 3 | 4 | 5 | 6 | 7 | 8 | 9 | 10 | 11 | 12 | 13 | 14 | 15 | 16 | 17 | 18 | TOTAL |
|---|---|---|---|---|---|---|---|---|---|---|---|---|---|---|---|---|---|---|---|---|
| Santiago Luna | Round 1 | 4 | 6 | 3 | 5 | 3 | 4 | 4 | 5 | 2 | 4 | 4 | 3 | 5 | 5 | 4 | 2 | 4 | 5 | 72 |
| Spain | Round 2 | 3 | 4 | 4 | 4 | 3 | 5 | 5 | 4 | 3 | 4 | 5 | 3 | 4 | 5 | 4 | 4 | 4 | 4 | 72-144 |
| Barry Lane | Round 1 | 3 | 4 | 5 | 5 | 3 | 3 | 4 | 4 | 3 | 3 | 5 | 3 | 4 | 5 | 4 | 3 | 5 | 5 | 71 |
| England | Round 2 | 3 | 4 | 5 | 3 | 4 | 5 | 4 | 4 | 3 | 3 | 5 | 5 | 3 | 4 | 4 | 4 | 5 | 5 | 73-144 |
| Philip Walton | Round 1 | 3 | 4 | 4 | 4 | 4 | 5 | 4 | 4 | 4 | 4 | 5 | 3 | 4 | 3 | 5 | 6 | 3 | 3 | 72 |
| Ireland | Round 2 | 4 | 5 | 4 | 4 | 4 | 5 | 4 | 4 | 3 | 4 | 4 | 3 | 5 | 3 | 4 | 4 | 4 | 4 | 72-144 |
| Marc Farry | Round 1 | 3 | 4 | 4 | 5 | 3 | 4 | 4 | 3 | 3 | 4 | 4 | 3 | 3 | 4 | 5 | 5 | 5 | 4 | 70 |
| France | Round 2 | 4 | 4 | 5 | 4 | 3 | 5 | 5 | 5 | 3 | 3 | 5 | 3 | 4 | 4 | 4 | 4 | 4 | 5 | 74-144 |
| Silvio Grappasonni | Round 1 | 3 | 3 | 5 | 3 | 3 | 4 | 4 | 5 | 3 | 4 | 5 | 3 | 5 | 5 | 4 | 3 | 5 | 4 | 71 |
| Italy | Round 2 | 3 | 4 | 5 | 4 | 3 | 5 | 5 | 4 | 3 | 4 | 5 | 3 | 4 | 3 | 5 | 5 | 4 | 4 | 73-144 |
| Ricky Willison | Round 1 | 3 | 5 | 4 | 3 | 4 | 4 | 5 | 4 | 3 | 4 | 4 | 4 | 5 | 4 | 4 | 4 | 4 | 4 | 72 |
| England | Round 2 | 3 | 4 | 6 | 4 | 4 | 5 | 3 | 5 | 3 | 4 | 4 | 4 | 3 | 4 | 4 | 3 | 4 | 5 | 72-144 |
| David Feherty | Round 1 | 3 | 4 | 4 | 5 | 3 | 5 | 4 | 4 | 2 | 4 | 7 | 4 | 4 | 4 | 5 | 5 | 5 | 5 | 77 |
| N. Ireland | Round 2 | 3 | 5 | 4 | 4 | 2 | 4 | 5 | 4 | 2 | 4 | 4 | 3 | 4 | 3 | 4 | 4 | 4 | 4 | 67-144 |
| Sam Torrance | Round 1 | 3 | 5 | 5 | 4 | 4 | 3 | 5 | 5 | 3 | 3 | 6 | 3 | 3 | 4 | 4 | 5 | 3 | 4 | 72 |
| Scotland | Round 2 | 4 | 4 | 5 | 3 | 3 | 4 | 5 | 3 | 3 | 4 | 4 | 3 | 6 | 5 | 5 | 3 | 4 | 4 | 72-144 |
| Bob Estes | Round 1 | 4 | 5 | 4 | 3 | 3 | 5 | 4 | 4 | 3 | 4 | 5 | 4 | 4 | 5 | 4 | 4 | 4 | 4 | 73 |
| USA | Round 2 | 3 | 5 | 5 | 4 | 4 | 4 | 4 | 4 | 2 | 4 | 5 | 3 | 3 | 5 | 4 | 4 | 4 | 4 | 71-144 |
| Woody Austin | Round 1 | 3 | 4 | 4 | 4 | 3 | 4 | 5 | 4 | 3 | 4 | 5 | 4 | 4 | 5 | 4 | 4 | 4 | 4 | 72 |
| USA | Round 2 | 4 | 5 | 3 | 4 | 3 | 4 | 4 | 4 | 3 | 4 | 5 | 4 | 5 | 4 | 5 | 4 | 4 | 4 | 73-145 |
| Steve Elkington | Round 1 | 2 | 4 | 4 | 4 | 3 | 6 | 5 | 4 | 4 | 4 | 5 | 3 | 4 | 5 | 6 | 3 | 5 | 4 | 75 |
| Australia | Round 2 | 3 | 4 | 4 | 4 | 5 | 4 | 5 | 4 | 2 | 4 | 4 | 3 | 4 | 5 | 4 | 3 | 4 | 4 | 70-145 |
| Craig Parry | Round 1 | 3 | 4 | 3 | 4 | 3 | 5 | 4 | 5 | 3 | 4 | 5 | 3 | 4 | 4 | 6 | 4 | 5 | 5 | 74 |
| Australia | Round 2 | 3 | 4 | 5 | 4 | 3 | 5 | 5 | 4 | 2 | 4 | 5 | 3 | 3 | 4 | 4 | 4 | 4 | 5 | 71-145 |
| Jose Coceres | Round 1 | 3 | 4 | 4 | 4 | 4 | 5 | 4 | 4 | 3 | 4 | 5 | 3 | 4 | 4 | 4 | 4 | 4 | 5 | 72 |
| Argentina | Round 2 | 4 | 4 | 4 | 4 | 2 | 4 | 5 | 4 | 3 | 5 | 4 | 3 | 4 | 4 | 5 | 3 | 5 | 6 | 73-145 |
| Jose Rivero | Round 1 | 3 | 6 | 5 | 3 | 3 | 4 | 6 | 4 | 3 | 4 | 5 | 4 | 4 | 4 | 4 | 4 | 4 | 4 | 74 |
| Spain | Round 2 | 2 | 5 | 5 | 3 | 3 | 4 | 4 | 5 | 3 | 4 | 3 | 4 | 4 | 4 | 4 | 4 | 6 | 4 | 71-145 |
| Fuzzy Zoeller | Round 1 | 3 | 4 | 4 | 4 | 3 | 4 | 5 | 4 | 3 | 4 | 5 | 3 | 4 | 4 | 3 | 4 | 4 | 5 | 70 |
| USA | Round 2 | 4 | 4 | 4 | 5 | 3 | 4 | 5 | 4 | 3 | 4 | 5 | 4 | 4 | 4 | 5 | 4 | 4 | 5 | 75-145 |
| Lee Westwood | Round 1 | 3 | 5 | 4 | 4 | 3 | 5 | 4 | 4 | 3 | 4 | 5 | 3 | 4 | 4 | 4 | 4 | 4 | 4 | 71 |
| England | Round 2 | 4 | 5 | 4 | 4 | 3 | 5 | 5 | 5 | 3 | 4 | 5 | 3 | 4 | 4 | 5 | 3 | 4 | 4 | 74-145 |
| Peter O'Malley | Round 1 | 4 | 4 | 3 | 4 | 3 | 5 | 5 | 5 | 3 | 4 | 5 | 4 | 4 | 4 | 4 | 5 | 3 | 4 | 73 |
| Australia | Round 2 | 3 | 4 | 4 | 4 | 3 | 5 | 6 | 5 | 3 | 4 | 4 | 4 | 4 | 5 | 4 | 4 | 3 | 3 | 72-145 |
| Sean Murphy | Round 1 | 3 | 4 | 3 | 5 | 4 | 4 | 5 | 4 | 3 | 4 | 5 | 3 | 4 | 4 | 5 | 5 | 5 | 6 | 76 |
| USA | Round 2 | 2 | 4 | 4 | 4 | 2 | 4 | 5 | 4 | 3 | 4 | 4 | 4 | 5 | 4 | 4 | 4 | 4 | 4 | 69-145 |
| *Warren Bladon | Round 1 | 3 | 4 | 4 | 4 | 4 | 4 | 5 | 4 | 3 | 3 | 5 | 4 | 4 | 4 | 4 | 5 | 5 | 5 | 73 |
| England | Round 2 | 4 | 5 | 4 | 4 | 4 | 5 | 4 | 5 | 3 | 5 | 5 | 3 | 4 | 4 | 4 | 3 | 3 | 4 | 73-146 |
| Andrew Coltart | Round 1 | 2 | 4 | 4 | 5 | 3 | 5 | 7 | 5 | 3 | 4 | 4 | 3 | 4 | 3 | 4 | 4 | 4 | 4 | 72 |
| Scotland | Round 2 | 3 | 4 | 5 | 4 | 3 | 4 | 4 | 3 | 4 | 4 | 6 | 4 | 4 | 4 | 4 | 4 | 6 | 4 | 74-146 |
| Malcolm Mackenzie | Round 1 | 3 | 5 | 4 | 4 | 3 | 4 | 5 | 4 | 2 | 3 | 5 | 2 | 4 | 4 | 5 | 4 | 4 | 6 | 71 |
| England | Round 2 | 3 | 4 | 4 | 3 | 3 | 5 | 5 | 5 | 3 | 4 | 7 | 4 | 4 | 4 | 4 | 4 | 5 | 4 | 75-146 |
| Ross McFarlane | Round 1 | 5 | 4 | 4 | 5 | 2 | 4 | 5 | 4 | 3 | 4 | 4 | 4 | 4 | 6 | 4 | 3 | 4 | 4 | 73 |
| England | Round 2 | 3 | 4 | 4 | 4 | 3 | 5 | 6 | 5 | 3 | 4 | 4 | 3 | 4 | 4 | 5 | 4 | 4 | 4 | 73-146 |

| HOLE | | 1 | 2 | 3 | 4 | 5 | 6 | 7 | 8 | 9 | 10 | 11 | 12 | 13 | 14 | 15 | 16 | 17 | 18 | |
|---|---|---|---|---|---|---|---|---|---|---|---|---|---|---|---|---|---|---|---|---|
| PAR | | 3 | 4 | 4 | 4 | 3 | 5 | 5 | 4 | 3 | 4 | 5 | 3 | 4 | 4 | 4 | 4 | 4 | 4 | 4 TOTAL |
| Steve Jones | Round 1 | 3 | 4 | 5 | 4 | 4 | 4 | 5 | 4 | 3 | 4 | 4 | 4 | 4 | 3 | 4 | 5 | 5 | 4 | 73 |
| USA | Round 2 | 4 | 5 | 5 | 4 | 3 | 4 | 4 | 4 | 3 | 4 | 5 | 4 | 3 | 4 | 5 | 4 | 5 | 3 | 73-146 |
| Yoshinori Kaneko | Round 1 | 3 | 4 | 4 | 4 | 3 | 4 | 5 | 4 | 3 | 4 | 5 | 4 | 4 | 4 | 5 | 4 | 5 | 5 | 73 |
| Japan | Round 2 | 3 | 4 | 4 | 4 | 3 | 4 | 5 | 4 | 3 | 4 | 4 | 3 | 6 | 4 | 5 | 5 | 4 | 4 | 73-146 |
| Peter Senior | Round 1 | 4 | 4 | 6 | 4 | 4 | 4 | 5 | 4 | 4 | 4 | 4 | 3 | 4 | 3 | 4 | 4 | 5 | 4 | 74 |
| Australia | Round 2 | 3 | 4 | 4 | 4 | 4 | 4 | 6 | 4 | 3 | 4 | 6 | 3 | 3 | 4 | 3 | 4 | 4 | 5 | 72-146 |
| Paul Eales | Round 1 | 3 | 4 | 4 | 4 | 4 | 5 | 4 | 5 | 3 | 4 | 5 | 3 | 4 | 5 | 5 | 3 | 5 | 3 | 73 |
| England | Round 2 | 4 | 4 | 5 | 4 | 3 | 4 | 4 | 4 | 2 | 3 | 6 | 3 | 5 | 4 | 4 | 4 | 5 | 5 | 73-146 |
| Tony Johnstone | Round 1 | 3 | 4 | 5 | 4 | 3 | 4 | 5 | 4 | 3 | 4 | 5 | 3 | 4 | 4 | 4 | 3 | 4 | 4 | 70 |
| Zimbabwe | Round 2 | 3 | 5 | 4 | 4 | 3 | 5 | 3 | 4 | 3 | 4 | 5 | 5 | 6 | 4 | 4 | 5 | 4 | 5 | 76-146 |
| Davis Love III | Round 1 | 3 | 4 | 4 | 4 | 3 | 5 | 4 | 4 | 3 | 4 | 5 | 3 | 4 | 3 | 5 | 4 | 5 | 5 | 72 |
| USA | Round 2 | 3 | 4 | 5 | 4 | 4 | 4 | 5 | 4 | 3 | 4 | 4 | 3 | 3 | 4 | 6 | 5 | 3 | 6 | 74-146 |
| Bill McColl | Round 1 | 3 | 5 | 6 | 4 | 3 | 4 | 4 | 4 | 3 | 4 | 5 | 3 | 5 | 4 | 5 | 4 | 4 | 4 | 74 |
| Scotland | Round 2 | 4 | 5 | 4 | 4 | 4 | 4 | 4 | 4 | 2 | 5 | 4 | 4 | 4 | 4 | 4 | 4 | 4 | 4 | 72-146 |
| Terry Price | Round 1 | 5 | 5 | 5 | 4 | 3 | 4 | 5 | 4 | 4 | 4 | 5 | 3 | 4 | 5 | 4 | 4 | 5 | 4 | 77 |
| Australia | Round 2 | 3 | 4 | 4 | 4 | 4 | 4 | 6 | 4 | 2 | 4 | 4 | 3 | 4 | 4 | 4 | 4 | 5 | 3 | 70-147 |
| Justin Leonard | Round 1 | 4 | 5 | 5 | 4 | 3 | 5 | 5 | 6 | 3 | 4 | 6 | 4 | 3 | 4 | 5 | 5 | 4 | 4 | 79 |
| USA | Round 2 | 3 | 4 | 4 | 4 | 3 | 4 | 4 | 3 | 2 | 3 | 5 | 3 | 4 | 4 | 4 | 4 | 6 | 4 | 68-147 |
| Satoshi Higashi | Round 1 | 3 | 4 | 4 | 5 | 3 | 4 | 4 | 4 | 4 | 4 | 4 | 3 | 3 | 6 | 5 | 5 | 6 | 4 | 75 |
| Japan | Round 2 | 4 | 4 | 4 | 4 | 4 | 4 | 5 | 4 | 3 | 5 | 5 | 3 | 4 | 4 | 4 | 4 | 3 | 4 | 72-147 |
| Per-Ulrik Johansson | Round 1 | 3 | 4 | 5 | 3 | 3 | 4 | 4 | 4 | 3 | 3 | 5 | 4 | 4 | 4 | 5 | 4 | 4 | 4 | 70 |
| Sweden | Round 2 | 3 | 5 | 5 | 4 | 3 | 5 | 6 | 4 | 3 | 4 | 5 | 4 | 5 | 4 | 4 | 4 | 4 | 5 | 77-147 |
| Gordon Brand Jnr | Round 1 | 3 | 4 | 4 | 4 | 3 | 5 | 3 | 6 | 4 | 4 | 5 | 4 | 3 | 3 | 5 | 4 | 4 | 4 | 72 |
| Scotland | Round 2 | 3 | 5 | 4 | 4 | 2 | 5 | 4 | 6 | 3 | 3 | 5 | 3 | 3 | 5 | 5 | 4 | 5 | 6 | 75-147 |
| Gary Player | Round 1 | 3 | 4 | 4 | 4 | 3 | 5 | 5 | 4 | 3 | 4 | 4 | 3 | 4 | 4 | 4 | 4 | 5 | 4 | 71 |
| South Africa | Round 2 | 3 | 3 | 4 | 4 | 3 | 6 | 4 | 4 | 3 | 5 | 4 | 4 | 5 | 5 | 4 | 5 | 5 | 5 | 76-147 |
| Ian Woosnam | Round 1 | 3 | 4 | 6 | 4 | 3 | 3 | 6 | 4 | 2 | 4 | 5 | 4 | 3 | 5 | 4 | 4 | 8 | 3 | 75 |
| Wales | Round 2 | 4 | 4 | 4 | 4 | 3 | 4 | 5 | 4 | 2 | 5 | 4 | 3 | 4 | 4 | 4 | 5 | 5 | 5 | 72-147 |
| Steen Tinning | Round 1 | 4 | 4 | 4 | 4 | 4 | 5 | 5 | 4 | 3 | 3 | 4 | 3 | 4 | 4 | 4 | 4 | 5 | 4 | 72 |
| Denmark | Round 2 | 3 | 4 | 4 | 5 | 3 | 4 | 6 | 4 | 3 | 4 | 7 | 3 | 4 | 4 | 4 | 4 | 5 | 4 | 75-147 |
| Colin Montgomerie | Round 1 | 3 | 4 | 5 | 4 | 3 | 4 | 5 | 5 | 3 | 3 | 4 | 4 | 4 | 4 | 4 | 4 | 4 | 6 | 73 |
| Scotland | Round 2 | 3 | 4 | 4 | 4 | 3 | 5 | 4 | 5 | 3 | 5 | 5 | 3 | 6 | 4 | 4 | 4 | 4 | 4 | 74-147 |
| Anders Forsbrand | Round 1 | 3 | 4 | 4 | 4 | 3 | 5 | 5 | 3 | 3 | 4 | 5 | 3 | 4 | 4 | 6 | 5 | 6 | 4 | 75 |
| Sweden | Round 2 | 3 | 5 | 4 | 4 | 4 | 4 | 5 | 4 | 2 | 4 | 5 | 2 | 3 | 4 | 6 | 5 | 4 | 4 | 72-147 |
| *Steve Allan | Round 1 | 3 | 4 | 5 | 4 | 3 | 3 | 5 | 4 | 3 | 5 | 6 | 4 | 5 | 5 | 4 | 4 | 4 | 4 | 75 |
| Australia | Round 2 | 3 | 4 | 5 | 4 | 3 | 5 | 5 | 6 | 2 | 3 | 6 | 2 | 3 | 4 | 5 | 4 | 4 | 4 | 72-147 |
| Mark Litton | Round 1 | 2 | 4 | 4 | 3 | 3 | 5 | 5 | 4 | 3 | 4 | 5 | 3 | 4 | 4 | 4 | 4 | 6 | 5 | 72 |
| Wales | Round 2 | 4 | 5 | 3 | 4 | 3 | 6 | 5 | 4 | 3 | 4 | 5 | 4 | 5 | 4 | 5 | 3 | 4 | 4 | 75-147 |
| Andrew Sherborne | Round 1 | 3 | 3 | 4 | 4 | 3 | 4 | 3 | 5 | 3 | 4 | 4 | 4 | 5 | 4 | 5 | 5 | 5 | 5 | 73 |
| England | Round 2 | 3 | 4 | 4 | 4 | 4 | 6 | 5 | 4 | 2 | 4 | 6 | 3 | 4 | 4 | 4 | 4 | 4 | 5 | 74-147 |
| Steven Bottomley | Round 1 | 4 | 4 | 4 | 4 | 4 | 5 | 6 | 4 | 3 | 4 | 6 | 3 | 4 | 5 | 3 | 4 | 4 | 5 | 76 |
| England | Round 2 | 3 | 4 | 5 | 3 | 3 | 6 | 5 | 4 | 3 | 4 | 6 | 2 | 4 | 3 | 4 | 4 | 4 | 5 | 72-148 |
| Massimo Florioli | Round 1 | 3 | 5 | 3 | 3 | 3 | 4 | 6 | 4 | 3 | 4 | 5 | 3 | 5 | 4 | 4 | 4 | 3 | 4 | 71 |
| Italy | Round 2 | 3 | 4 | 5 | 6 | 4 | 5 | 5 | 5 | 4 | 5 | 4 | 3 | 3 | 4 | 4 | 3 | 5 | 5 | 77-148 |
| David J. Russell | Round 1 | 4 | 6 | 4 | 5 | 4 | 6 | 3 | 5 | 2 | 4 | 6 | 3 | 4 | 4 | 4 | 4 | 5 | 4 | 77 |
| England | Round 2 | 3 | 4 | 4 | 5 | 3 | 5 | 4 | 4 | 4 | 3 | 4 | 4 | 3 | 5 | 4 | 4 | 4 | 4 | 71-148 |
| Wayne Westner | Round 1 | 3 | 5 | 5 | 4 | 3 | 6 | 6 | 6 | 3 | 4 | 4 | 3 | 4 | 4 | 4 | 4 | 5 | 5 | 78 |
| South Africa | Round 2 | 3 | 4 | 4 | 4 | 4 | 4 | 5 | 4 | 4 | 3 | 4 | 3 | 4 | 3 | 4 | 4 | 5 | 4 | 70-148 |

| HOLE | | 1 | 2 | 3 | 4 | 5 | 6 | 7 | 8 | 9 | 10 | 11 | 12 | 13 | 14 | 15 | 16 | 17 | 18 | |
|---|---|---|---|---|---|---|---|---|---|---|---|---|---|---|---|---|---|---|---|---|
| PAR | | 3 | 4 | 4 | 4 | 3 | 5 | 5 | 4 | 3 | 4 | 5 | 3 | 4 | 4 | 4 | 4 | 4 | 4 | TOTAL |
| **Stephen Field** | Round 1 | 3 | 4 | 3 | 5 | 3 | 5 | 5 | 4 | 4 | 4 | 5 | 3 | 4 | 3 | 4 | 3 | 6 | 4 | 72 |
| England | Round 2 | 4 | 5 | 4 | 4 | 3 | 4 | 6 | 5 | 4 | 3 | 5 | 4 | 4 | 5 | 4 | 3 | 5 | 4 | 76-148 |
| **Hajime Meshiai** | Round 1 | 3 | 4 | 4 | 4 | 4 | 4 | 5 | 5 | 4 | 4 | 5 | 4 | 4 | 5 | 4 | 4 | 5 | 4 | 76 |
| Japan | Round 2 | 3 | 3 | 4 | 4 | 4 | 5 | 4 | 4 | 3 | 4 | 6 | 5 | 5 | 4 | 4 | 3 | 4 | 3 | 72-148 |
| **Antoine Lebouc** | Round 1 | 3 | 4 | 4 | 4 | 3 | 4 | 4 | 5 | 3 | 4 | 7 | 4 | 4 | 4 | 4 | 4 | 4 | 3 | 72 |
| France | Round 2 | 3 | 4 | 4 | 3 | 3 | 4 | 5 | 5 | 4 | 4 | 5 | 4 | 4 | 4 | 6 | 5 | 4 | 5 | 76-148 |
| **Gary Emerson** | Round 1 | 5 | 4 | 5 | 4 | 3 | 4 | 5 | 5 | 3 | 4 | 5 | 3 | 4 | 4 | 4 | 5 | 4 | 5 | 76 |
| England | Round 2 | 4 | 4 | 4 | 3 | 3 | 4 | 7 | 4 | 2 | 3 | 5 | 4 | 4 | 4 | 4 | 3 | 6 | 4 | 72-148 |
| **Stuart Cage** | Round 1 | 4 | 4 | 4 | 4 | 4 | 6 | 4 | 3 | 3 | 4 | 4 | 4 | 4 | 5 | 4 | 5 | 4 | 4 | 74 |
| England | Round 2 | 3 | 4 | 5 | 4 | 3 | 5 | 4 | 5 | 3 | 4 | 4 | 4 | 3 | 5 | 5 | 4 | 5 | 5 | 75-149 |
| **Tim Herron** | Round 1 | 4 | 4 | 5 | 4 | 3 | 4 | 5 | 4 | 4 | 4 | 4 | 4 | 4 | 4 | 4 | 4 | 4 | 5 | 74 |
| USA | Round 2 | 3 | 4 | 5 | 4 | 4 | 4 | 6 | 4 | 2 | 5 | 6 | 3 | 4 | 3 | 4 | 5 | 5 | 5 | 75-149 |
| **Jon Robson** | Round 1 | 2 | 4 | 5 | 5 | 3 | 4 | 5 | 5 | 3 | 4 | 4 | 3 | 4 | 5 | 5 | 5 | 5 | 4 | 75 |
| England | Round 2 | 2 | 4 | 4 | 4 | 4 | 4 | 4 | 6 | 3 | 4 | 5 | 4 | 4 | 4 | 4 | 4 | 5 | 5 | 74-149 |
| **\*Sergio Garcia** | Round 1 | 3 | 4 | 4 | 4 | 3 | 4 | 4 | 5 | 3 | 4 | 6 | 4 | 4 | 4 | 5 | 4 | 6 | 5 | 76 |
| Spain | Round 2 | 3 | 5 | 5 | 4 | 3 | 5 | 5 | 4 | 3 | 4 | 5 | 4 | 4 | 4 | 3 | 4 | 4 | 4 | 73-149 |
| **Thomas Bjorn** | Round 1 | 3 | 4 | 4 | 4 | 3 | 5 | 6 | 5 | 3 | 5 | 4 | 3 | 2 | 5 | 6 | 4 | 4 | 3 | 73 |
| Denmark | Round 2 | 3 | 5 | 4 | 4 | 3 | 6 | 4 | 5 | 3 | 4 | 7 | 4 | 4 | 4 | 4 | 3 | 4 | 5 | 76-149 |
| **Wayne Riley** | Round 1 | 4 | 4 | 4 | 4 | 2 | 4 | 4 | 5 | 3 | 3 | 5 | 4 | 4 | 4 | 4 | 4 | 6 | 5 | 73 |
| Australia | Round 2 | 3 | 4 | 4 | 3 | 3 | 4 | 7 | 5 | 3 | 4 | 6 | 3 | 5 | 4 | 5 | 5 | 4 | 4 | 76-149 |
| **Joakim Haeggman** | Round 1 | 3 | 4 | 6 | 4 | 3 | 5 | 4 | 4 | 3 | 3 | 4 | 3 | 4 | 4 | 5 | 4 | 5 | 4 | 72 |
| Sweden | Round 2 | 3 | 4 | 5 | 4 | 4 | 4 | 4 | 5 | 3 | 4 | 5 | 4 | 4 | 4 | 5 | 4 | 6 | 5 | 77-149 |
| **Diego Borrego** | Round 1 | 3 | 5 | 4 | 4 | 4 | 6 | 4 | 4 | 3 | 4 | 5 | 4 | 4 | 4 | 5 | 4 | 4 | 3 | 74 |
| Spain | Round 2 | 4 | 5 | 5 | 4 | 2 | 4 | 4 | 4 | 4 | 4 | 4 | 3 | 6 | 4 | 5 | 4 | 4 | 4 | 75-149 |
| **Iain Steel** | Round 1 | 3 | 4 | 5 | 4 | 3 | 4 | 5 | 4 | 3 | 4 | 4 | 3 | 4 | 4 | 5 | 4 | 4 | 5 | 72 |
| Scotland | Round 2 | 4 | 4 | 4 | 5 | 4 | 5 | 4 | 5 | 3 | 5 | 5 | 2 | 4 | 4 | 4 | 4 | 4 | 7 | 77-149 |
| **Fabrice Tarnaud** | Round 1 | 2 | 4 | 4 | 4 | 4 | 5 | 5 | 5 | 3 | 5 | 7 | 3 | 3 | 3 | 5 | 3 | 5 | 4 | 74 |
| France | Round 2 | 3 | 5 | 4 | 3 | 4 | 5 | 5 | 4 | 4 | 3 | 4 | 4 | 5 | 4 | 5 | 4 | 5 | 4 | 75-149 |
| **Andrew Oldcorn** | Round 1 | 3 | 4 | 4 | 4 | 3 | 5 | 5 | 4 | 3 | 5 | 4 | 4 | 4 | 5 | 5 | 5 | 6 | 4 | 77 |
| Scotland | Round 2 | 5 | 4 | 4 | 4 | 3 | 5 | 5 | 5 | 3 | 4 | 4 | 3 | 4 | 4 | 5 | 4 | 4 | 3 | 73-150 |
| **Jay Townsend** | Round 1 | 2 | 4 | 5 | 3 | 3 | 6 | 4 | 4 | 3 | 5 | 5 | 3 | 4 | 5 | 4 | 4 | 5 | 3 | 72 |
| USA | Round 2 | 3 | 5 | 4 | 4 | 3 | 4 | 5 | 3 | 3 | 5 | 5 | 3 | 6 | 4 | 5 | 4 | 7 | 5 | 78-150 |
| **Brian Watts** | Round 1 | 5 | 5 | 5 | 4 | 4 | 6 | 5 | 4 | 3 | 3 | 5 | 2 | 4 | 5 | 4 | 4 | 8 | 4 | 80 |
| USA | Round 2 | 4 | 4 | 3 | 3 | 3 | 3 | 5 | 5 | 3 | 4 | 5 | 3 | 4 | 4 | 4 | 5 | 4 | 4 | 70-150 |
| **Miguel Angel Jimenez** | Round 1 | 4 | 4 | 4 | 4 | 4 | 5 | 6 | 4 | 2 | 4 | 6 | 3 | 4 | 4 | 4 | 4 | 4 | 5 | 75 |
| Spain | Round 2 | 3 | 5 | 4 | 4 | 4 | 5 | 5 | 5 | 2 | 4 | 4 | 5 | 6 | 4 | 4 | 3 | 4 | 4 | 75-150 |
| **Robert Lee** | Round 1 | 3 | 4 | 3 | 4 | 4 | 6 | 5 | 4 | 4 | 3 | 5 | 4 | 4 | 4 | 6 | 4 | 5 | 5 | 77 |
| England | Round 2 | 3 | 4 | 4 | 4 | 4 | 5 | 5 | 4 | 3 | 4 | 5 | 3 | 5 | 3 | 4 | 4 | 4 | 5 | 73-150 |
| **Lee Janzen** | Round 1 | 4 | 3 | 4 | 4 | 3 | 4 | 4 | 5 | 3 | 3 | 6 | 3 | 4 | 5 | 4 | 4 | 5 | 6 | 74 |
| USA | Round 2 | 3 | 4 | 5 | 4 | 5 | 5 | 5 | 4 | 4 | 4 | 6 | 3 | 4 | 4 | 4 | 3 | 6 | 4 | 77-151 |
| **Paul Azinger** | Round 1 | 3 | 4 | 4 | 4 | 3 | 5 | 5 | 5 | 4 | 3 | 5 | 3 | 4 | 5 | 5 | 4 | 4 | 4 | 74 |
| USA | Round 2 | 4 | 5 | 4 | 4 | 3 | 4 | 5 | 5 | 4 | 3 | 6 | 3 | 4 | 4 | 6 | 3 | 6 | 4 | 77-151 |
| **Mats Hallberg** | Round 1 | 4 | 4 | 4 | 4 | 3 | 6 | 7 | 4 | 3 | 4 | 4 | 3 | 5 | 4 | 6 | 5 | 4 | 5 | 79 |
| Sweden | Round 2 | 3 | 5 | 5 | 4 | 4 | 5 | 5 | 4 | 2 | 4 | 5 | 3 | 4 | 4 | 4 | 3 | 4 | 4 | 72-151 |
| **Adam Mednick** | Round 1 | 3 | 4 | 5 | 4 | 3 | 5 | 5 | 4 | 3 | 4 | 6 | 3 | 3 | 4 | 6 | 4 | 4 | 5 | 75 |
| Sweden | Round 2 | 5 | 4 | 3 | 3 | 3 | 5 | 5 | 5 | 4 | 4 | 4 | 4 | 4 | 4 | 5 | 4 | 7 | 3 | 76-151 |
| **Bob Tway** | Round 1 | 3 | 4 | 4 | 5 | 3 | 5 | 5 | 4 | 3 | 4 | 5 | 3 | 5 | 5 | 5 | 4 | 6 | 6 | 79 |
| USA | Round 2 | 4 | 4 | 4 | 4 | 3 | 5 | 5 | 4 | 3 | 4 | 5 | 3 | 4 | 4 | 4 | 4 | 4 | 5 | 73-152 |

| HOLE | | 1 | 2 | 3 | 4 | 5 | 6 | 7 | 8 | 9 | 10 | 11 | 12 | 13 | 14 | 15 | 16 | 17 | 18 | |
|---|---|---|---|---|---|---|---|---|---|---|---|---|---|---|---|---|---|---|---|---|
| PAR | | 3 | 4 | 4 | 4 | 3 | 5 | 5 | 4 | 3 | 4 | 5 | 3 | 4 | 4 | 4 | 4 | 4 | 4 | TOTAL |
| Severiano Ballesteros | Round 1 | 3 | 4 | 5 | 4 | 3 | 6 | 4 | 5 | 3 | 4 | 4 | 3 | 5 | 5 | 5 | 3 | 4 | 4 | 74 |
| Spain | Round 2 | 3 | 4 | 4 | 5 | 2 | 5 | 5 | 5 | 4 | 5 | 5 | 4 | 4 | 4 | 4 | 4 | 6 | 5 | 78-152 |
| Ross Drummond | Round 1 | 2 | 4 | 7 | 4 | 3 | 5 | 5 | 4 | 4 | 4 | 6 | 3 | 4 | 4 | 5 | 5 | 5 | 4 | 78 |
| Scotland | Round 2 | 3 | 4 | 6 | 4 | 3 | 4 | 5 | 5 | 3 | 4 | 6 | 4 | 3 | 4 | 4 | 4 | 4 | 4 | 74-152 |
| Gary Brown | Round 1 | 3 | 4 | 6 | 5 | 4 | 4 | 4 | 4 | 3 | 4 | 6 | 3 | 4 | 4 | 4 | 4 | 4 | 4 | 74 |
| England | Round 2 | 4 | 5 | 5 | 5 | 3 | 5 | 5 | 6 | 3 | 4 | 6 | 4 | 4 | 4 | 4 | 4 | 4 | 5 | 80-154 |
| Paul Lawrie | Round 1 | 3 | 5 | 5 | 4 | 3 | 5 | 5 | 4 | 5 | 3 | 7 | 4 | 4 | 4 | 5 | 4 | 4 | 4 | 78 |
| Scotland | Round 2 | 3 | 4 | 5 | 5 | 4 | 6 | 5 | 4 | 4 | 4 | 6 | 4 | 3 | 4 | 4 | 3 | 5 | 4 | 77-155 |
| Kazuhiro Fukunaga | Round 1 | 3 | 5 | 3 | 3 | 3 | 4 | 6 | 6 | 4 | 4 | 7 | 3 | 4 | 4 | 7 | 3 | 4 | 3 | 76 |
| Japan | Round 2 | 3 | 4 | 5 | 4 | 3 | 5 | 5 | 7 | 5 | 4 | 6 | 4 | 4 | 4 | 4 | 4 | 4 | 6 | 81-157 |
| Ian Baker-Finch | Round 1 | 3 | 6 | 4 | 4 | 4 | 4 | 5 | 5 | 4 | 4 | 4 | 3 | 5 | 4 | 6 | 3 | 5 | 5 | 78 |
| Australia | Round 2 | 3 | 7 | 5 | 4 | 4 | 6 | 5 | 5 | 4 | 4 | 4 | 3 | 4 | 5 | 5 | 6 | 5 | 5 | 84-162 |
| Des Smyth | Round 1 | 3 | 4 | 6 | 4 | 3 | 5 | 4 | 5 | 3 | 3 | 4 | 3 | 3 | 4 | 5 | 4 | 5 | 4 | 72-DQ |
| Ireland | | | | | | | | | | | | | | | | | | | | |
| Michael Campbell | Round 1 | 3 | 4 | 4 | 3 | 3 | 6 | 4 | 4 | 3 | 5 | 4 | 3 | 5 | 5 | 6 | 4 | 4 | 5 | 75-DQ |
| New Zealand | | | | | | | | | | | | | | | | | | | | |
| Bernhard Langer | Round 1 | 3 | 5 | 4 | 4 | 4 | 5 | 5 | 5 | 3 | 3 | 6 | 3 | 3 | 4 | 5 | 4 | 5 | 4 | 75-WD |
| Germany | | | | | | | | | | | | | | | | | | | | |

# ROYAL LYTHAM
# AND ST. ANNE'S
# GOLF CLUB

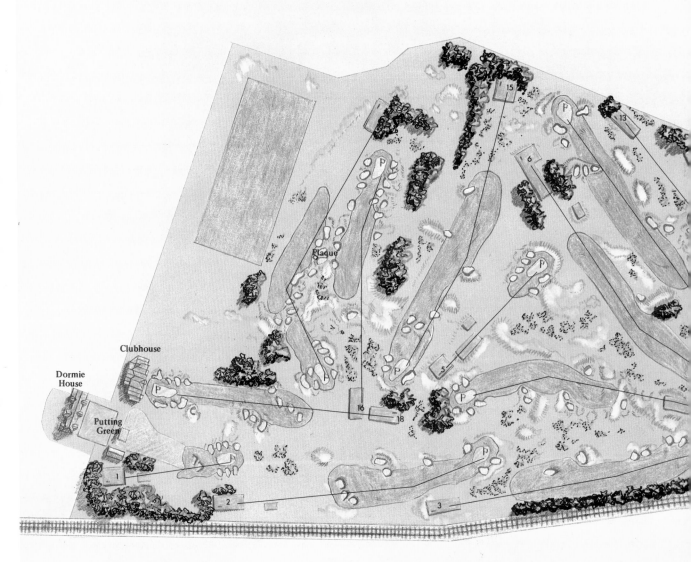